James Cary is a BBC sitcom·
Another Case of Milton Jones) an
of the General Synod for the Ch
lot of his life watching jokes (soi.   ... .o own) go horribly
wrong.

He runs a touring theatre company and performs. In 2017, he produced a 64-date tour of the UK of a show about Martin Luther and the 95 Theses, called *A Monk's Tale*, which ran for two weeks at the Edinburgh Fringe.

James is married with two children and lives in Somerset.

THE SACRED ART OF JOKING

James Cary

First published in Great Britain in 2019

Society for Promoting Christian Knowledge
36 Causton Street
London SW1P 4ST
www.spck.org.uk

British Library Cataloguing-in-Publication Data
A catalogue record for this book is available from the British Library

ISBN 978–0–281–08092–2
eBook ISBN 978–0–281–08093–9

1 3 5 7 9 10 8 6 4 2

Typeset by Manila Typesetting Company
Printed in Great Britain by Jellyfish Print Solutions

eBook by Manila Typesetting Company

Produced on paper from sustainable forests

Contents

Contents

Foreword

There are two types of people in the comedy business, or in any art form, probably. There are those who cling on to the few ideas they believe they own, bitter at the success of others. But then there are some, no less ambitious or hard-working, who want to share the joy of any treasure found, and even the technique of its discovery. These types love their art, often because they've worked long and hard down a hole themselves, and can't help celebrating when a diamond turns up. James Cary is one of these.

He is uniquely qualified to write this book. He has been familiar with Christian circles – whatever they are – for a long time. But he has also worked for many years at the coalface of comedy, sorting the dross from the combustible. Having worked with him, I know that he laughs out loud at good jokes. (Not a prerequisite for a job in our industry, by the way.) He has even helped me to excavate some of my particular 'gold', and to sort it from the Fool's Gold, and the even less valuable Idiot's Silver, that I've tried to get past him.

These are strange times. Institutions are crumbling, and methods of communication multiplying and updating continually. Religious views can be broadcast more easily than ever before, but then so too can anyone's offence. To be part of a debate, it seems you have to pull up a powder keg and sit down on it. Censorious religion and popular humour have not always been comfortable, er, bedfellows. But comedy is all about truth, and Christianity is supposed to be too.

Comedy is increasingly influential in a world that is distrustful of anything presented as fact. Yet authorities are often keen to water down words in case they cause trouble. Laughing is sometimes the only weapon we have against those who would impose their rules on us.

Creating funny stuff is not an exact science. Comic success is like a many-layered lasagne, the recipe for which is lost each time it's served up. Like other crafts, done well it looks simple and achievable by anyone who has the tools. It's really not. Its shifting alchemy is barely understood by those who do it for a living.

Here, using examples from history, the history of comedy and the Bible, James Cary stylishly explains why Christianity can and should provide the ultimate context for being able to laugh.

After all, faith is like a joke in that it divides those who get it from those who don't, and so – assuming Christians haven't got completely the wrong end of the stick – they should be able to laugh long, loud and into eternity!

Milton Jones

Preface

Only once have I attempted actual journalism. You be the judge of how well it went.

It was 2008. I had been asked to interview Ben Elton for a now defunct Christian magazine called *Third Way*, for which I used to write a column. As a sitcom writer myself, they thought I might bring some insight to the piece.

I jumped at the chance. Elton is a comedy hero, co-writer of classic comedy *Blackadder*, entire episodes of which I had memorized by the end of my teenage years. Doing my best to look like a serious journalist rather than a grinning fanboy, I met Elton in a café on Shepherd's Bush Green.

The conversation was interesting enough, especially for a comedy geek like me. We talked a little about Ben Elton's latest novel, which he was promoting. The unremarkable interview was transcribed and edited. Very little journalism was required on my part. No one was talking nominations for Pulitzers.

After a few weeks, the interview was duly printed and circulated. And it made headlines. As I hunted down a copy of *The Times* in which Ruth Gledhill had broken 'the story', I tried to remember what Elton had said that was in any way controversial, shocking or factually untrue.

When I found a copy of the article, I saw they had plucked out Elton's comments on how, in his opinion, the BBC would allow jokes about vicars to pass but not jokes about imams. He said things were so bad that it was difficult to use even common sayings while writing and rehearsing a sitcom:

I wanted to use the phrase 'Muhammad came to the mountain' and everybody said, 'Oh, don't! Just don't! Don't go there!' . . . It was nothing to do with Islam, I was merely referring to the old proverb, 'If the mountain won't come to Muhammad, Muhammad must go to the mountain.' And people said, 'Let's just not!' It's incredible.[1]

Was the BBC afraid of Islam? Ben Elton was unavailable for comment, having already returned to Australia, where he lives for at least part of the year. So the 'journalist' responsible for the original article was dredged up and summoned to the *Newsnight* studio. This was, I have to admit, rather exciting as I found myself sitting opposite Jeremy Paxman along with some other comedians discussing the issues around comedy, religion and offence. I did not feel the need to agree with or defend Elton's comments, although neither did I want to say that I felt his comments were inappropriate or untrue.

This all rumbled on for another 24 hours and went global. I took part in a BBC World Service phone-in show called *World Have Your Say*, which included in its panel Anjem Choudary, subsequently imprisoned in HMP Belmarsh for inciting people to join ISIS. He was at pains to point out that he and his wife had a good sense of humour.

The next day, almost as quickly as it erupted, the storm blew itself out. I decided that proper journalism wasn't for me.

Ship of Fools

I should not have been surprised at the furore about religion and comedy. A couple of years earlier, I had unwittingly found myself in the press through a subversive Christian comedy website called Ship of Fools. They were running a competition trying to find the best but also the most offensive religious jokes. The top ten of each kind were to be read out at the Greenbelt Festival, a large Christian arts festival (think Latitude with a few prayers and dog collars). Having been involved in the festival for a few years, and

---

[1] <www.theguardian.com/media/2008/apr/02/bbc.television3>.

as someone with an interest in this area, I agreed to be involved and read some of these jokes out.

When I saw the jokes, however, I was astonished at how imaginatively offensive they were. I'm reluctant even to write them here and have managed almost to blot them from my memory, but to give you a flavour, there were jokes that somehow sexualized Christ's wounds. I was scandalized. Not only could I not read the jokes out, I felt I couldn't even be in the same tent as they were being read out. In a very slow week during silly season, this was also deemed worthy of being reported in a national newspaper.

This came hot on the heels of the *Jerry Springer: The Opera* debacle, in which Jesus Christ was portrayed as being an adult in a nappy and saying that sometimes he felt 'a bit gay', all bathed in impressive levels of swearing. We look at this show later in this book.

All of the above was several years PT (pre-Twitter). Recent experience shows that, far from enabling discussion of the issues among friends in a dispassionate way, social media has polarized opinions. It has fanned the flames of dissent and turned moral outrage into performance art which, ironically, must not be questioned or critiqued.

The need to discuss issues surrounding religion, comedy and offence have never been more pressing. We live in a world in which the staff of *Charlie Hebdo* were brazenly shot dead in broad daylight for the production of satirical cartoons. At the same time, social media, rolling news and the need for compelling clickbait have all made that discussion even harder to conduct in a rational, constructive or good-humoured way.

Where's your sense of humour?

We think, rightly, that having a sense of humour is incredibly important. We Brits especially pride ourselves on having a sense of humour. We consider it essential that someone can take a joke. Dating profiles often specify a GSOH (Good Sense of Humour).

We are suspicious of politicians who seem to be overly serious – and are quick to give a free pass to ones who joke around. At weddings, we think it important to take the time to humiliate the bridegroom with a dirt-dishing best man's speech. The groom has to just sit there and take it, while the rest of the room cringes.

This practice has morphed into the 'celebrity roast', a format popular on American television. The White House Correspondents' Dinner is a version of that where the president is fair game, although Donald Trump was criticized for not attending the first Correspondents' Dinner of his presidency. And yet Trump used humour a great deal on the campaign trail, much to the annoyance and outrage of his opponents.

People giving speeches at dull conferences love to start off with a joke. We like greetings cards with funny pictures and captions. We engage in practical jokes, hoaxes and April Fool's Day antics. We think comedy is really important, and yet it can so easily go horribly, embarrassingly, toxically, career-endingly wrong, especially in the realm of religion.

And that, dear reader, is why you are holding this book in your hands. We need to think seriously about the issues surrounding comedy, religion and offence in a measured, informed and good-humoured way.

If we learn those lessons, maybe we can break the cycle of misconstrued jokes, media outrage, hysterical punditry, reactionary commentary and grovelling apologies.

But I doubt it.

Instructions

This is a book about comedy and why it goes wrong, from the baffled look and the eye-roll to public shaming and death threats.

I suggest you read Parts 1, 2 and 3 of this book in that order. This will seem obvious to most readers. The instruction could be construed as insulting. If so, apologies. No offence is intended on this occasion. There is material in this book that I expect will offend some readers. I hope I can justify why that's okay but, of course, you may not appreciate the arguments being put forward if you turn to the chapters of greatest interest first.

Plenty of readers may already have thumbed straight past this page. In an attempt to arrest their attention as they rush past, I have called this chapter 'Instructions' rather than 'Introduction'. But also, I'd like to explain briefly how this book works beyond 'open it and start reading'. It looks as if you've already got the hang of that.

In Part 1, we look at the basic anatomy of a joke and how comedy is considerably more complex than it first appears. I argue that the actual words of the joke may not tell you whether a particular joke should have been told or not.

In Part 2, we see how jokes work – or fail to work – in the religious realm, with particular reference to Christianity. This is partly because that is my experience, but also because it is still the dominant religion in the West and the basis of our culture and morality. I will argue that the causing of offence is a poor guide as to whether a particular joke should have been told or not.

With all of the above in mind, we will launch into Part 3, which gives some practical out-workings of these principles with specific references to famous cases in which jokes have gone horribly wrong. Or, arguably, gone right and caused outrage and chaos.

Instructions complete. I'm pleased to say that an Allen key was not required.

Part 1

A GOOD SENSE OF HUMOUR

1

It's funny because it's true

Freud said that the essence of the comic was the conservation of psychic energy. But then again Freud never played second house Friday night at the Glasgow Empire. (Ken Dodd)

Whom would you rather listen to on the subject of comedy, Sigmund Freud or Ken Dodd? Academics, psychologists, linguists, theologians and social scientists have their theories about comedy. But wouldn't you rather listen to Ken Dodd, not least because he went out on stage night after night and made audiences laugh for hours on end?

Nothing is less funny than theories of comedy. As E. B. White famously said, 'Explaining a joke is like dissecting a frog. You understand it better but the frog dies in the process.' Most of us have been in that situation where you crack a joke and receive blank looks. Try to explain the joke and you will only make matters worse. Bemusement will turn to pity. Never go back.

The task before us, however, is to understand comedy better so that we can see how it goes wrong. Therefore, we need to have a stab at some kind of overarching theory of comedy.

This, I believe, is impossible. Comedy is by nature subversive. It tweaks your nose and taps you on the wrong shoulder. It rings your doorbell and runs. It defies exhaustive explanations, because it undermines everything around it. That's what makes comedy so anarchic and hard to control.

If a social anthropologist presents some Grand Unified Theory of Comedy in a lecture hall, someone will stand up and say, 'What about knock knock jokes?' or demand to know how limericks or innuendo fit in. The academic will scrabble for an answer, realizing a chink has been found in the armour. As it all starts to fall apart, people will start to giggle, and not know why. Which is in itself funny. But it is also hard to say why.

I do not propose to get bogged down by academic theories on 'humour' or Freud's ideas about psychic energy. Let's go with some widely accepted maxims among comedians and comedy writers I've worked with over the past 20 years. One key element is this:

Comedy is based on truth. In order for a joke to work, it has to have a kernel of truth at the heart of it.

Observational comedy

This is clearly true of what is often called 'observational comedy'. A comedian points out things we all do in the bathroom or the bedroom, and habits we have formed that we hadn't noticed were universal. And this is funny. I'm not entirely sure why, but it's funny because it's true. If the observations weren't true, we wouldn't be laughing. This is the world of Michael McIntyre in the UK and Jerry Seinfeld in the USA.

Not everyone laughs at such comic observations. In fact, some comedians are very snobby about observational comedy, commenting that it is merely pointing things out. It's hard to argue with this. That is what it is. Common subjects that some comedians might consider overused or 'hack' would be highlighting the differences between men and women or cats and dogs. Cult comedians like Stewart Lee can be very funny in condemning this straightforward form of comedy. Ironically, their jokes about observational comedy are in themselves observations about comedians. For some reason that makes it okay. There we are. Comedy is hard to define. I did tell you that earlier.

Satire

The moment comedians start being rude about people rather than habits, pets or things, we are in the realm of satire, which is another type of comedy that clearly relies on telling the truth. Or at least a grotesque version of it. The satirist doesn't invent facts or motives. He or she takes a small truth and exaggerates it to the point of absurdity for comic effect.

Look at the Gerald Scarfe cartoons on the opening titles of *Yes, Minister*. The noses are very long and the bodies are out of shape, but they are recognizable and based on the actual appearance of the actors. The satire of the show is based on the truth of the impossibility of government and democracy, trying to square the eternal circle of 'popularity' vs 'doing the right thing'.

Satire also relies on another kind of truth: the truth of a morality that assumes injustice, cruelty and hypocrisy are wrong. The grubby individual truths of government ministers, bishops, journalists and TV personalities are held up to the greater truths of justice, mercy and integrity. We make jokes about MPs fiddling their expenses because that is based on the truth that some are doing it – and the truth that it is wrong.

Sitcoms

Truth may be the key for stand-up comedy and satire, where comedians are talking about or depicting real people or situations. But what about sitcoms which are entirely fictional? *Yes, Minister* is clearly only quasi-fictional because it is based on recognizable aspects of government, MPs and civil servants. What about *The Simpsons*? Or *Porridge*? Or *Mrs Brown's Boys*?

These sitcoms also rely on truth. The characters, situations and stories have to be believable. They have to have a truth to them. Or a 'ring of truth'. Or 'truthiness', a word popularized by American comedian Stephen Colbert.[1] Characters and situations

---

[1] There is some dispute about whether Colbert coined the word 'truthiness' or merely popularized it.

must sound plausible. Sometimes, to aid this believability, they are based on real people.

The legendary sitcom *Fawlty Towers* was based on a real hotel that John Cleese stayed at, where he encountered a highly strung proprietor who, at one point, was convinced a briefcase contained a bomb, grabbed it and hurled it outside into the car park. Cleese stayed on at the hotel in order to observe this man and Basil Fawlty was born. He is a character you have no trouble believing would beat his car with the branch of a tree or goosestep in front of German guests.

'Truth is stranger than fiction' is a well-worn cliché, but like most hackneyed phrases it's broadly true. When advising new writers in the creation of sitcoms, I remind them they can push characters to greater extremes than they might first think. In a quest for plausibility, sitcom characters can easily become bland and unremarkable, which is not what you want. Although TV heightens the persona, we live in a world in which Gordon Ramsay, Simon Cowell, Christine Hamilton and Geoffrey Boycott actually exist. Sitcom characters can be larger than life, but still believable.

Science fiction

A sitcom character and situation can be pure invention but must have that same quality of 'truthiness' and believability, even if you have an absurd situation like a man marooned in space years in the future, as in Grant and Naylor's *Red Dwarf*. In that show, the main characters are the last human alive, a humanoid cat, a hologram and an android. But the characters have to behave within believable parameters.

We don't need to like the characters in question or even identify with them. We just need to recognize them. Many of us know an Alf Garnett from *Till Death Us Do Part* (or *All in the Family*'s Archie Bunker in the USA). We do not need to agree with their views, merely believe people exist who espouse those views. The same goes for Edina in *Absolutely Fabulous*. She behaves like a child, but we are prepared to believe that people like that exist in the fashion industry.

The Logic Police

Good comedy characters, then, are based on truth. What they get up to must be truthful to that character. It's frustrating to see a character in a TV show or movie do something that makes no sense in that situation. When I'm editing sitcom scripts, I sometimes refer to the Logic Police.[2]

The most obvious example is the stereotype of bad horror films in which stranded teenagers voluntarily decide to stay in a clearly haunted and creepy house in the woods. Watching the movie, you're thinking that any rational person would not go near the place, let alone stay the night. Immediately the dishonesty of the story has broken the spell. Someone call the Logic Police.

Characters can do irrational and illogical things as long as we believe that they would. No one would beat a broken-down car with a tree branch. But the genius of *Fawlty Towers* is that we have no problem believing that Basil Fawlty would do just that.

You can't handle the truth

The internet is full of quotations of dubious origins. There is a particularly good one on humour attributed to famous comedian Victor Borge, who apparently said: 'Humour is something that thrives between man's aspirations and his limitations. There is more logic in humour than in anything else. Because, you see, humour is truth.' If comedy is based on truth, we can begin to see why it can easily go wrong. Because the truth hurts.

It's why jokes are often bitter-sweet, or 'close to the bone', especially in satire. Hypocrisy that we have learned to live with or ignore has been highlighted.

---

[2] See <http://sitcomgeek.blogspot.com/2015/01/the-logic-police.html>.

A good sense of humour

Good sitcoms are truthful. They depict people we recognize in our lives, showing them to be ludicrous or laughable. Fortunately, most people are blind to this most of the time, especially when it concerns their own failings or comic flaws. If there's a character in a sitcom who is exactly like your boss at work, your boss will most likely find it funny too because he or she knows someone exactly like that, blissfully unaware of the reflection closer to home. No one exemplifies this exact situation better than David Brent in *The Office* (or Michael Scott in the US version), a character whom everyone recognizes. But no one thinks, 'That's me.'

Ironically we also know this to be true, and it's funny when this is the joke. One occasion springs to mind from a Dame Edna Everidge television show. The self-proclaimed megastar and creation of Barry Humphries was asked about what 'she' liked and didn't like. In reply, she talked at length about how repulsive she finds it when men dress up as women, unable to understand why anyone would find that funny. Which was, of course, hilarious.

Because of this blindness, we can get away with a lot more jokes than we think we can. But we can already see how comedy can so easily go wrong when the truth hits home and the listener experiences a sense of humour failure.

As we have said earlier, clichés have a grain of truth in them. Jokes rely on clichés and stereotypes, and this can easily be the cause of offence, as we will see in the next chapter.

2

An Englishman, an Irishman and a Scotsman . . .

I f someone says, 'An Englishman, an Irishman and a Scotsman . . .' you know exactly what's coming: a joke. The three men are either in the jungle about to be eaten by cannibals or in an aeroplane about to jump out. What happens next?

The Englishman is usually up first as the straight man, establishing the rules of this particular world. Then the Scotsman goes next, sometimes with a half-joke implying the Scots are, in some way, miserly or partial to alcohol. Then the Irishman blunders in and is the joke proper, usually based around his idiocy.

Irish people have every right to take offence at these jokes. But bear in mind the same kind of jokes are told all over the world – including Ireland, where they change the Irishman to a man from Kerry. The Kerryman is the Irishman's dunce.

The Americans used to make those same jokes about Poles, whom they considered to be joke-worthily stupid. This mantle was taken on by George W. Bush, who became the butt of many jokes, although the gags were broadly similar to the ones told about Ronald Reagan. Americans also tell jokes about the Irish, but those jokes are mostly about drinking and drunkenness, the same jokes that the Brits might tell about the Scots.

A world of stereotypes

The Brits also tell jokes about Germans, referring to their supposed lack of sense of humour and their insistence on taking the best sun-loungers by hotel swimming pools by putting their towels on them before breakfast.

The Brits think the French are obsessed with food, shut down for lunch and apparently don't wash. You can see more stereotypes in *Muppets Most Wanted* in Ty Burrell's portrayal of Frenchman Jean Pierre Napoleon, who drives a tiny car, drinks coffee from microscopic cups and stops work at 2 p.m.

In the land of jokes, the Dutch are all on drugs, are hyper-liberal and all speak English perfectly. The Spaniards take long siestas and are cruel to bulls and donkeys. Italians are portrayed as cowards in war.[1] These types are combined in a joke that has circulated the internet for many years. It runs as follows:

> Heaven is where the police are British, the lovers French, the mechanics German, the chefs Italian, and it is all organized by the Swiss.

> Hell is where the police are German, the lovers Swiss, the mechanics French, the chefs British, and it is all organized by the Italians.

But all of the above is just the Anglo-American perspective. Travel the world and you will find other stereotypes, sometimes manifest in football chants, which often tap into the most basic prejudices. To the Dutch, the Germans are bicycle thieves. Whenever the two nations play each other at football, the Dutch will hold up signs that ask for the return of their bicycles. This is because, at the end of the Second World War, the Germans beat a hasty

---

[1] I remember, at a young age, being told a joke that Italian tanks were fitted with more reverse gears than forward ones.

retreat from the Netherlands, commandeering motor vehicles of all kinds – and eventually bicycles. Perhaps the pettiness and desperation of this theft is the reason it has become lodged so firmly in the Dutch mind.

Professional stereotypes

Comedy stereotypes are not limited to nationality. Professions present some buttons that are easily pressed. Think of cab drivers, whose views are usually considered to be, let's say, traditional and heavily informed by speech-based radio. Lawyers have the habit of ending up on the winning side and charging a lot of money for their time. Politicians are considered to be habitual liars and on the take. Builders famously never turn up when they say they will, always have another job on somewhere else, take three sugars in their tea and charge more than the original estimate.

In the 1990s, there was quite a spate of 'blonde' jokes in which the gag was, clearly, that women with blonde hair were considered to be unintelligent. As I continue to march into this comedy minefield some readers will be wincing at these sweeping and offensive generalizations.

One should barely need to say that there are plenty of smart Irish people, sober Scots, funny Germans, progressive cabbies and punctual builders. So why perpetuate these stereotypes in jokes? Is it immoral or irresponsible to do so?

Every joke has a context and we will address that in future chapters. But here we should note that Englishman, Irishman and Scotsman jokes are not really about Englishmen, Irishmen or Scotsmen. These kinds of jokes are a handy, recognizable format that enables a particular kind of gag to work. These jokes are clearly not being told against the Irish. Or Kerrymen. Or Poles. That stereotype is grabbed because it's a useful shorthand.

But why do we even need shorthand? Why is that useful? Shakespeare would say that 'Brevity is the soul of wit.' Not only is this true, it is also pleasingly succinct.[2] Jokes tend to work when they are punchy and efficient, for reasons we shall see. It will then become obvious why we need stereotypes and shorthand, and why this can easily go wrong.

---

[2] In fact, Shakespeare did not say this line. He wrote it for his character Polonius in *Hamlet*. This is significant, as we shall see later in the book. Also, the line might not even be original to Shakespeare, but might have been common parlance. Moreover, the pleasingly short line is actually part of a longer line: 'Since brevity is the soul of wit and tediousness the limbs and outward flourishes, I will be brief.' Which rather contradicts Polonius's point. But perhaps it's a joke at his expense.

3

How jokes work
(without killing a frog)

Aristotle's *Poetics* is about the workings of drama, tragedy and comedy. It's a timeless classic. There is only one problem. It is written on separate rolls of papyrus and only the first part, concerned with tragedy and epic, survives. The second papyrus, about comedy, is missing. Perhaps he never wrote it and the lack of a second papyrus was illustrating a point he made in the first part about suspense. Maybe it's a slow burn.

It is possible that Aristotle wanted to disappoint those eager to make jokes and improve their craft in that area. Read his *Nicomachean Ethics* and you will read disparaging words about those who like jokes. He even suggests laws might need to be passed against this sort of thing.[1] If you believed in reincarnation, you'd swear he came back as a TV critic for a broadsheet newspaper.

Out of the mouths of babes

There is a much simpler way to work out the mechanics of jokes than rummaging through ancient texts: listen to children. They love jokes. They latch on to them early in their development. They try to remember them, and get them wrong. They make up new jokes. And get them very wrong. It's adorable, obviously. But a train-wreck for the comedy purist.

---

[1] *Nicomachean Ethics*, Book Four, Chapter 8.

If you listen to how they get it wrong and as you teach them how to get it right, you realize you already know how jokes work (but thanks for buying my book, anyway). You can teach children the basic mechanics by using some very common terms. They are: the set-up; the punchline; and 'getting it'. We will look at those in turn.

The set-up

The set-up is often the majority of the joke, in which the listener is given *all* the key information. This might be posed as a question, such as 'Why did the golfer wear two pairs of trousers?', or presented as a short story: 'A horse goes into a bar and goes up to the barman . . .'

Anything that's not relevant or necessary should be left out. We don't need to know about what else the golfer is wearing or what the name of the bar is. If we know it's a joke, we're already trying to work out the punchline. And when the pay-off comes, we want a nice resolution that takes account of all the significant information presented.

Setting up a joke is, therefore, quite difficult. It needs to be grammatically correct and coherent. It should move along smoothly[2] and make clear what the actual joke is. You don't want listeners to be worried about whether they've spotted the joke or whether they have understood it correctly. This is where stereotypes are so helpful. They rapidly convey clear crucial information.

Confusion is the enemy of comedy. Imagine doing a blindfolded taste test. The food is normally less enjoyable because you're apprehensive about what it is going to be. It could be disgusting, or it could be a trick designed to make you look foolish.

---

[2] Unless the joke is that it is agonisingly slow or repetitive, like a shaggy dog story, in which case the slowness of the set-up *is* the joke. A good example would be the 'Two Soups' sketch in *Victoria Wood As Seen On TV* or Ronnie Corbett's stories in the chair in *The Two Ronnies*, where it takes him a long time to get to the actual joke.

The uncertainty is not fun. It's the same with jokes. You want the elements of the joke to be clear. A golfer is wearing two pairs of trousers. That's it. That's all you need to know.

The joy of formats

This is why joke formats are useful. They rapidly establish what sort of joke this is going to be. Doubt and confusion are decreased. Someone says, 'Knock knock' and you know what comes next. 'Who's there?' and we can all relax into the joke.[3]

There are many jokes set at the pearly gates of heaven. When we hear those words, we know that the scene about to unfold is going to be based around whether the person at the gates talking to St Peter has lived a good life or a bad life. Maybe he or she has some cunning way of exploiting a loophole, if it's a joke about a lawyer.

Stand-up comedians tend to avoid joke formats because they rightly feel the urge to be more original. They've had more practice at telling jokes and setting them up correctly without relying on popular formats. They are very careful about every word they say, and know exactly what information is being imparted to their audience. For the amateur, the joke format is a useful starter kit, like stabilizers for your comedy bicycle.

The punchline

So, let us say that our joke is in full flow. It is being told. The set-up is in progress and we have reached the punchline.

> The golfer wore two pairs of trousers in case he got a hole in one! Badoom-tish!

If the set-up is lighting the fuse, the punchline is the bang. It's where one element meets another and there is a reaction.

---

[3] Although a little piece of you dies because you know it's a 'knock knock' joke, the most tiresome and contrived of all joke formats.

The golfer joke is a very old one, but it's neat. Nothing is wasted. We're not wondering about the golfer's opponent, the clubs or the caddy. There are two elements to the joke: a golfer and two pairs of trousers. These combine the double meaning of 'hole in one'. That's the joke. And it's right at the end, which makes it funnier. It needs no further explanation or caveats.

Misdirection

Punchlines rely on misdirection. They are the jolt that rapidly pulls you away from where you thought the sentence was headed towards an unexpected destination. The result is a comic juxtaposition. Two things that don't belong together are now right next to each other. They are incongruous.

For me, this is the most convincing explanation of how most jokes work. That's why double acts are often different shapes and sizes from each other. There's incongruity in front of you before they've started the routine. Normally one is trying to get on with 'the act' and the other is messing about.

Let's take a moment here to think about the 'theory of incongruity', which is well established in the mostly unreadable annals of comedy theory. Søren Kierkegaard called these comic explosions 'contradictions', building on ideas put forward by two German philosophers, Schopenhauer and Kant, men who rank among the least funny in the history of Western civilization. How pleasingly incongruous that such dour writers should understand the essence of comedy. And then not use it.

It puts me in mind of a joke in the 'lightbulb' style: how many Germans does it take to screw in a lightbulb?

It's a popular joke format because we know it's nothing to do with someone needing a light turned on. We're not asking why the bulb is broken. We know the joke will portray a group of people in an unflattering but light-hearted way.

This joke is about Germans. What will the joke be? Our brains start racing ahead to the punchline. Maybe it'll refer to the Second

World War. Or the precision of German engineering. Or beach towels. If it's a Dutch joke, it might involve bicycles. The set-up suggests it is going to be a national stereotype joke, which it is – but not quite in the way that we're expecting.

Enough teasing. Let's have the whole joke now:

How many Germans does it take to screw in a lightbulb?
One. They're efficient and not very funny.

The answer of 'One' is a let-down, because that is all it takes for a lightbulb to be changed in normal life. What's going on here? The joke is the explanation. Germans are famously efficient. But they are also famous for not having a very good sense of humour, which is why the punchline is just three words, 'not very funny'. The joke is that in being so efficient and not screwing in the light-bulb in a comical way, they have actually ruined the joke.

It's a good gag, nearly killed by the speculation and explanation. Is the frog nearly dead? Almost. We've not yet looked at the 'getting it' part. We will do that in the next chapter, which is crucial to understanding how jokes go wrong.

4

How jokes go wrong

You know a joke has gone wrong when, after telling it, the joker feels obliged to say 'Get it?' This is normally accompanied by a forced grin. It's painful to watch. It's obvious we didn't get the joke. It misfired. The question is: why?

It may have been an established tried-and-tested joke but told incorrectly. Maybe the joker said, 'Why did the tennis player wear two pairs of trousers?' That's not going to work, is it? It has to be a golfer. We've all winced as friends in the pub and relatives round the dinner table make a mess of a perfectly decent joke. Everyone's wanting it to work, but it gets muddled and key information is omitted.

The error is corrected but it's too late. It's all been ruined and people look anxiously into their glasses or offer more cauliflower. The joke can't be retold. The surprise of the punchline has gone. It was a damp squib. And we hope that someone can pipe up with a new joke to restore the equilibrium of the universe.

Incomplete information

Another likely problem is that the joke was told correctly but the listener has never heard of the expression 'hole in one'. He or she knows nothing about golf and has incomplete knowledge, and so 'doesn't get it'. This is common with children, whose experience of the world is slight. They haven't had long enough to gather much information or have some prejudices firmly entrenched.

There is a very old and pleasing joke that runs as follows: 'When is a door not a door? When it's ajar.' Unless you know the word 'ajar' means 'slightly open', that joke will be baffling. That said, it has the rhythm of a joke, so a child might instinctively guffaw before saying 'I don't get it.'[1]

In my house when I was growing up, if anyone used to say, 'It's a matter of opinion', my mother would usually chime in with the punchline: 'Said the man with a wooden leg'. She would explain that a pinion is some kind of rod or pin. I have never used this word in adult life but it does technically exist. And so the joke is technically funny. But it never made me laugh as a child. The only thing that I did enjoy was that my mother persisted with the joke for many years, at which point it became a different kind of joke about persistence with a joke that will never be funny to the listener.

Bisons and basins

Another reason for a punchline failure is questionable incongruity. A pun relies on one word sounding like another but the two having different meanings. But if it doesn't really sound that similar to begin with, the joke is weak. There's an old joke that runs:

What's the difference between a buffalo and a bison?
You can't wash your hands in a buffalo.

I did warn you. It's a groaner because it depends on the similarity of the words 'bison' and 'basin'. They don't really sound that similar in most English dialects so it's a very weak joke. It might be slightly funnier in Birmingham, where 'bison' sounds more like 'basin'. But only slightly.

---

[1] Jokes undoubtedly have a magical musical quality and rhythm that could and probably should be the subject of another book, a book I fully intend not to write. Jason Hazeley – who is both a superb comedy writer and a musician – spoke about this in Episode 56 of *Sitcom Geeks*: <www.comedy.co.uk/podcasts/sitcom_geeks/episode_56/>.

You had to be there

Sometimes you try to explain a funny moment to someone, perhaps a calamity at the office which made everyone laugh. But in the explanation it doesn't seem so funny any more. In those situations, you might bail out on the story with the excuse 'You had to be there'.

This phenomenon illustrates the complexities of jokes rather well. In the moment the original hilarious calamity happened, a few things took place at once. Those who witnessed them put together the incongruity in their minds very quickly, and it was hilarious. Later, when you try to piece it all back together, you find it impossible to recreate and convey the complex factors that collided in such a way as to make it funny to someone who wasn't there. You really did have to be there.

Jokes are fickle friends. They promise much and yet they turn out to be very hard to get right. We can understand why it's often said that in learning a language the last thing you learn is the humour. Unless you have mastered the language or the customs or assumptions of that culture, you will struggle to 'get it'.

What makes things even worse is that sometimes the joke doesn't go wrong, but right. But it still has a negative reaction. We will look at that next.

5

Punched by a punchline

Punchlines are extremely tricky to get right. I've sat around for many hours crafting them. It's an odd way to make a living. My children can't quite believe it pays the bills, but there it is. The world needs jokes. And I write them.

Punchlines need to have a rhythm and flow to them. They need to come as late in the joke as possible. Ideally, they need to be at the very end. And they need to be a nice surprise or twist.

Being told a joke is a bit like taking part in a lucky dip or pulling a cracker. You don't know what you're going to get, but it's going to be a surprise. Hopefully a nice one. It'll be some miniature cards or a sewing kit. If you're lucky, it'll be a set of those tiny screwdrivers that are brilliant for tightening up a pair of wobbly spectacles. It's not going to be a diamond ring. Nor is it going to be a mouldy sprout. You have a rough idea of what's coming.

This is why setting the right expectations is crucial. The set-up is everything. Sometimes, the punchline is obvious. There is a natural form of words that *has* to be the pay-off, but the trick is making it flow naturally from the set-up. You have to erase words that send the listener in the wrong direction. But there is a right wrong direction and a wrong wrong direction.

I have done this in the most painstaking detail on the radio shows I have written with comedian Milton Jones. It's a *Goons*-style show with a silly story and lots of jokes. It is counter-intuitive, but often we have to make certain parts less funny or interesting to make it look as if we're going to do a joke about one thing when we're actually going to do a joke about something else, so that the punchline is the right kind of surprise. A tiny screwdriver rather than a mouldy sprout.

It's a kind of magic

Jokes aren't very different from magic tricks. You're trying to control where the audience is looking and what they are thinking – and then reveal they had it all wrong. The final flourish of the trick reveals that the card that's been there the whole time in plain sight is not what you thought it was. Or the real Queen of Hearts has been in your coat pocket all along. The incongruity creates a fizz of joy and delight.

Punchlines are just that. They are a final flourish of word or action that reveals the audience had it wrong all along. In that moment of the punchline, people immediately see how and why. All being well, they laugh.

But sometimes they don't. Sometimes they gasp, or tut. They might even be angry. If you're a famous comedian or a public figure, they might tweet their rage. It might have been caught on camera. Your career might be in the balance. It might be over. And the joke hasn't even gone wrong. It's worked. If anything, it's worked too well. How does that come about?

Sitcom moments

There is a comedy cliché that actually happened to me recently. I turned on a tap in a washroom and the water came out so fast it splashed on to my trousers. Naturally, it looked as though I'd had an unfortunate accident and I was humiliated.

The point here is that punchlines sometimes behave like that tap. Jokes are meant to bring joy and laughter. The punchline should be a nice surprise. But it might present more as a nasty shock. It's too much to handle in one go. The punchline has punched too hard. The tap was opened and water gushed out.

I was expecting water, but not this much this fast. It's all over my trousers and I'm not happy.

Even if you're listening to a comedian who is notoriously dark or transgressive, a joke can arrive that's just too much. Or a best man's speech is even filthier or more revealing about the groom than anticipated and it's all very embarrassing. The joke went right, but it's gone wrong.

The anvil in the glove

It might not be the joke itself but the language used in the joke that means the punchline has not been anticipated. The set-up to the joke successfully painted one picture, and the revelation of the punchline was something ugly or sinister. A joke about children playing turns into something violent or inappropriate. Theoretically, the joke worked. And while some are unoffended and find the comic incongruity hilarious, others are horrified and express dismay. Possibly the largest group are those who are offended but laugh anyway. But they may then resent being made to laugh in this way.

There is a Twitter account called Forest Friends (<@forest_fr1ends>) which creates scenes out of small children's toys. They are usually homely scenes of sweet-looking rabbits in domestic situations. The captions, however, are shockingly offensive, telling a tale of dysfunction and depravity using very crude language. The incongruity is enormous. Many would find it offensive, but others revel in the inappropriateness of it. The fact that it's *so* offensive would make it all the funnier for others. As punchlines go, they punch very hard. Some relish that. Many do not.

Sometimes, the joke itself is the sudden escalation of intensity. This presents its own problems, which we will return to later.

Nothing but the truth

We're beginning to see how fraught with difficulty the business of telling jokes is. There are so many ways to go wrong.

Sometimes jokes go wrong because they're sending the audience in the wrong wrong direction. And sometimes they send them in the right wrong direction and go right, but still go wrong because the joke was a shock rather than a surprise.

Perhaps the joke has dared to say the unsayable. If comedy is based on truth, then the joke may have uncovered something that had been suppressed, or reopened a wound that for some is too painful. These are jokes that don't get a laugh, but a wince. But others may find them hilarious. Whose reaction is right? And whose is wrong? The answers are far from simple.

6

Where's the line?

What is one of least funny things in the world? A disdainful presenter of *Newsnight* reading out a contentious joke to a comedian being hauled over the coals for some quip. After delivering the gag without intonation, joy or relish, the presenter leans forward and says to the accused, 'Is that supposed to be funny?'

No. It isn't funny. The presenter knows this and has contributed to its unfunniness by reading it out intentionally badly and, crucially, out of context, in a cold and mirthless news studio. The news programme may also have gone out of its way to invite another person to sit there and be upset or offended by the joke all over again.

Drawing the line

The news media – and religious groups – continually crave immutable rules about jokes. A joke can apparently be treated like a sample that is sent away to the lab to be tested. When I go swimming at my local gym, a pool attendant might dip a beaker in water and take it away, presumably checking for chlorine or urine. (Whenever they do that, I always feel the urge to cry out, 'It wasn't me.' I normally resist this urge.)

The same cannot be done for jokes. They should not be ripped out of their original context and sent off to the Bureau of Acceptable Jokes for testing. Jokes may look innocuous written down but were toxic at the moment of delivery. Equally, they may look vile written down but seem strangely appropriate at the time. The joke itself is not a reliable indicator of whether that joke should or should not have been told.

ABC of comedy

Let us see the complexities in play here. Assume we have three people involved in a joke: Adam, Barbara and Colin. Adam is telling the joke to Colin. And the joke is about Barbara's hair. She's having a bad hair day. The exact wording of the joke doesn't matter and we don't want to get hung up on that for now. Perhaps the joke is comparing her hair to that of Rod Stewart, Action Man, Pink, Boris Johnson, Donald Trump, Tina Turner or Albert Einstein. Right now, it doesn't really matter. How is Colin going to react? And how would we react?

It partly depends on whether Barbara is in the room and able to hear the joke. We moderate our speech in front of people for a variety of reasons, a mix of tact, kindness and cowardice. But this is just the beginning. Adam, Barbara and Colin are operating in a context of varied interwoven relationships.

Adam and Colin

Adam, the joker, has a relationship with Colin, the listener. But what is that relationship? That will determine how the joke is heard or construed. Are Adam and Colin lifelong buddies? Are they brothers? Are they colleagues? Are they two men who have just met in a bar? In a gay bar? Are they fellow Members of Parliament? Are they two men who've just met in the stands at a county cricket match? Is Adam a headmaster on Speech Day and Colin a schoolboy? Or is Adam the schoolboy in detention and Colin the headmaster, who is married to Barbara? Is Adam a stand-up comedian and Colin a member of the audience? Or is Colin the comedian and Adam a heckler? Is the stand-up comedy gig at a tiny backroom club? Or an arena? Is it televised or livestreamed?

Adam and Barbara

Adam is telling a joke *about* Barbara. Does Adam know Barbara personally? That will affect how the joke is heard. Are Adam and Barbara close colleagues? Business rivals? Siblings? Is Barbara Adam's mother? Or sister? Is Barbara a leading hair expert? Or a pop star who's known for dressing well? Or who makes a concerted attempt to dress provocatively badly? Or outrageously like Lady Gaga?

Is Barbara the president of a country? Is it a rich country like Sweden or a poor country like El Salvador? Or is Barbara an immigrant in a rich country doing a menial job? Is Barbara on death row, having killed her husband and children? Is Barbara a fictional character? Is she a sitcom character? Or a cartoon character from the 1930s, like Betty Boop?

Are they all in a comedy club, where Barbara has been heckling all night from the front row? Or is she another stand-up comedian who was on just before Adam? Are they friends? Or rivals? Or ex-lovers? All of these different situations affect how Colin will hear, process and respond to the joke.

In some cases, Colin will deem the joke inappropriate. Let's say Adam is a colleague and making disparaging remarks about Barbara, a poorly paid immigrant who has just finished cleaning the office. Colin might find Adam's joke to be mean-spirited. Colin, of course, might be a jerk and find it hilarious. An onlooker – let's call her Daphne – might be appalled at Adam and Colin. Or not, if she knows for a fact that Barbara has been stealing from her. The permutations are endless.

Similarly, Barbara might be the president of a country that has just dropped bombs on innocent civilians. In this instance, Colin might find jokes about her to be rather tame. Barbara is a vile dictator and you're doing jokes about her hair, Adam?

Colin and Barbara

Of course, Colin has his own relationship with Barbara. Colin might have voted for President Barbara and be in favour of the war that caused those bombs to be dropped, so Adam should shut the hell up. Jokes are a minefield. (Like the one that President Barbara has ordered to be laid in her war of conquest. That Barbara is just the worst.) Barbara may have passed laws prohibiting jokes in which she is criticized or satirized in public. So this innocuous hair joke is a way of sticking it to 'the man'. Or woman, in this case.

Barbara might be Colin's beautiful and adoring wife who is now being belittled by Adam, the stand-up comedian. In which case, Colin might be angry. Or both Barbara and Colin might have agreed before the night began that her hair is a disaster, that sitting at the front of a comedy gig will invite comment and they're just going to roll with the punches.

So, was this joke about Barbara's bad hair an act of cruelty, observation, satire or good-natured banter? That *entirely* depends on who is saying the joke, to whom and where. The actual words of the joke are not going to tell you whether the joke was suitable or in good taste. Let me say that again in a new paragraph with a very long title.

If you're a journalist and you are skim-reading this book then please make sure you read the following paragraph at the very least

The actual words of the joke are not going to tell you whether the joke was suitable or in good taste. I labour this point because journalists, news presenters, pundits and lobbyists consistently make this mistake. I have been asked the question 'Where is the line?' many times in interviews about which jokes are acceptable and which are not. If I do TV, radio, podcast or magazine interviews promoting this book, I will be asked that many times. The notion persists that there must be a yardstick or benchmark against which to measure jokes. But there isn't. Context is king.

So, journalist, if you're still reading this, please stop taking jokes out of context and transposing them to an overlit, sterile news studio. Stop making a point of reading out that joke slowly and badly, as if it were evidence in court. Please don't do this in front of a spokesperson for a lobby group who feels aggrieved by the joke. None of this is helpful or useful.

But all of the above will continue to happen, and I will probably be invited to take part in them. This is a shame because the misunderstanding of jokes has increasingly serious consequences.

7

Why jokes are no laughing matter

If you tell a joke in the pub, misread the room, get it wrong and cause offence, you may invoke criticism, arguments or jokes at your expense. Opening your wallet to buy drinks to remedy the situation may alleviate the problem considerably. Plus you have all evening to talk it out and make amends. Your relationships may never be quite the same again, but no permanent record of the joke was made and it will be largely forgotten.

The public square is less forgiving. Your comment, tweet, status update or soundbite will exist somewhere for ever. It can be used against you when the original context has been long forgotten. Only now are we coming to terms with these new forms of technology that once seemed transient and social. They have been shown to be permanent.

The jokes about Facebook used to be that it was the place where people posted pictures of their pets, their children and their lunch. Now the jokes are about how you are being constantly monitored and misled, and your conversations about anything mildly controversial could lose you friends. Your joke about Brexit or Trump or Jesus could evoke howls of dismay from people you used to joke with in the pub. You may be unfriended. You may be fired.

The twitchfork mob
When people are appointed to high office, their opponents, or journalists looking for an angle, will trawl through their Twitter feed looking for any hint of political incorrectness, jokes in poor

taste or presumed agreement with such jokes by the retweeting of them. This can cause embarrassment or hasty apologies (except in the case of Donald Trump). Someone may even resign a job before he or she has started it.

This was the case for Toby Young in early 2018, when he was appointed to the board of the Office for Students.[1] The 'twitch-fork mob' pulled out past tweets and links to articles he had written in the past. These were thrown in his face and he was publicly shamed for his espousal of contrarian views for the sake of a discussion (and personal income).

Social shaming and resignations are just the beginning. Joke tweets can trigger visits from the police and land you in prison. This naturally invites a binary innocent–guilty approach to comedy which is not helpful, even if it's legally necessary. Remember, *the actual words of the joke are not going to tell you whether the joke was suitable or in good taste*. We have seen that the context surrounding the joke is normally so impossibly complex that any verdict on the legality of a joke, and whether it constitutes 'hate speech', is not safe.

Twitter joke trial

What is more worrying is that our legislators, lawyers and judges are incapable of understanding even the most basic of jokes in the simplest of contexts. Take the case of Paul Chambers. On 6 January 2010, worried about disruption from cold weather at Robin Hood Airport (now called Doncaster Sheffield Airport) in South Yorkshire, Chambers tweeted: 'Crap! Robin Hood airport is closed. You've got a week and a bit to get your shit together otherwise I'm blowing the airport sky high!!'

It's not a great joke. In fact, it's barely a joke, more an attempt at being light-hearted. Nothing happened when Chambers tweeted this. He was obviously joking. The context made that obvious.

---

[1] <www.spectator.co.uk/2018/01/the-real-reason-im-a-target-for-the-twitchfork-mob/>.

But the retrospective discovery of this tweet triggered a visit by the anti-terror police.

Incredibly, Chambers was arrested and charged with 'sending a public electronic message that was grossly offensive or of an indecent, obscene or menacing character contrary to the Communications Act 2003'. A few months later, he was found guilty at Doncaster Magistrates' Court, fined £385 and ordered to pay £600 costs. The tweet cost Chambers £1,000. And his job.

It took a public campaign with high-profile comedians like Stephen Fry, Al Murray and Graham Linehan, a failed appeal at Doncaster Crown Court, two appeals to the High Court and two and a half years of the legal process for common sense to prevail. One argument put forward by John Cooper QC was that if Chambers' tweet had been 'menacing' so was John Betjeman's poem about his plea for friendly bombs to fall on Slough. Perhaps the estate of Betjeman should be sued by Slough Borough Council.

Pug dogs

This case is not an isolated incident. Mark Meechan, aka Count Dankula, made a video of his girlfriend's pug dog which he had trained to do a Nazi salute whenever he said '*Sieg heil*'. This video is deeply offensive as it also contains the repetition of the phrase 'Gas the Jews'. But it was still a joke. We will look at the details at play in Part 3, but the result was the police arrested Meechan in February 2017, and a year later he was found guilty in a Scottish court of law for the crime of hate speech.

These cases are not confined to the UK. In 2016 in Canada, comedian Mike Ward was fined $42,000 by the Quebec Human Rights Tribunal for a joke made six years earlier at the expense of Jérémy Gabriel, a young disabled singer. The joke was not particularly funny, and extremely unkind. But would it have been okay if it was only quite unkind and extremely funny? Understanding comedy and the importance of context has never been more important.

So where does this leave Adam, Barbara and Colin? One of these could have sent a tweet and been arrested. The stakes are high for everyone, not just comedians. But let's say that Adam is a stand-up comedian. In this brave new world of television, YouTube and camera-phones, what does he need to be prepared for?

8

Rules of engagement

Sir David Frost knew a fair bit about television. He once joked that 'Television is an invention that permits you to be entertained in your living room by people you wouldn't have in your home.'

Television is an intrusive medium. Responsible broadcasters like the BBC know that. Therefore, the comedy piped into your home on the BBC is slightly different from the comedy you might find in a late-night, booze-fuelled comedy club. Comedians behave according to the medium and the situation. When they're being filmed in front of 3,000 people for a TV show that may be seen by millions – and repeated for a decade – they are very careful about what they say.

Those same comedians know that they can change their tone in a comedy club where people have gone to the effort of leaving their home to buy a ticket. These are more likely to be 'comedy fans' who are more adept at understanding the complex relationships at play. They understand that not everything that is said is meant. And not everything that is said is remembered, since there is normally a fair amount of alcohol circulating too.

This does not mean that comedy clubs are amoral and the comedian can say anything he or she likes. Everyone in the room brings a moral framework into the club with them. It is not a completely 'safe' environment where anything goes and the audience laugh at everything without ever taking offence. Any working comedian will tell you stories of fights that have broken out because of offence taken at jokes and comic misunderstand-ings. The alcohol can exacerbate this. Sometimes bouncers do have to eject troublesome audience members. Sometimes com-edians are not invited back. Nonetheless, comedy clubs are places where the jokes can be harsher or more experimental than their TV equivalents. Or, at least, they have been.

Not so smart now

Smart phones have changed all this. The presence of a smart phone in a comedy club has serious consequences. Comedians like Chris Rock have banned them from gigs, insisting fans leave them at home or lock them in specially provided pouches.[1] What's the main concern here? Is it piracy? Are they trying to stop their new material appearing on the internet almost immediately? It's probably partly that. But the likes of Chris Rock aren't losing any ticket sales because of wobbly footage on a smart phone. They are more concerned that the phone takes the audience out of the moment, distracts them from following the comedian's painstak-ingly rehearsed train of thought.

I would be more worried about the fact that, in comedy clubs, smart phones can kill. Sorry to change the mood so swiftly, but let us consider the possibilities. Audience members can capture a joke on video and immediately upload it on to the internet. That joke can then be viewed completely out of context anywhere in the world straight away.

The joke may seem innocuous at first, but what if it is, say, an obscene joke about, say, a prophet from, say, one of the world's favourite religions? That clip can be viewed in Kabul, Tehran and Karachi. There could be riots, as there were for certain Danish cartoons and the publication of *The Satanic Verses*. People will

---

[1] <www.cbc.ca/news/canada/british-columbiachris-rock-comedian-phone-ban-vancouver-first-time-1.4287189>.

die. Suddenly, keeping the joke in its original context seems not just important but essential for the preservation of human life.

Would the comedian have told that joke in a public square in Tehran? It seems unlikely. Does that mean no one should be able to tell that joke anywhere? Probably not. But given you can't tell that joke in public in Tehran, does that mean it's right that you cannot tell it in a comedy club in Manchester? We will return to this later in the book. For now, the main point is: context is crucial. This is critical in helping us understand how appropriate or misjudged the joke was.

Pull back and reveal

Let's lighten up for a moment. Context is not just important for the jokes. Sometimes, it *is* the joke. Comedy writers normally call these 'pull back and reveal' jokes. A scene is taking place that makes sense, but isn't especially funny or surprising. But then the camera pulls back and reveals that the scene is taking place in an incongruous situation.

In an episode of the short-lived gem of a sitcom, *Spaced*, Tim (Simon Pegg) is angrily berating a customer for liking *The Phantom Menace*, a movie that *Star Wars* purists really hated. After a while, we pull back and reveal whom he's talking to: a young child. Tim's rage is now comically inappropriate. The incongruity is funny – even more so as he doesn't back down or moderate his speech for the next 15 seconds, sending the child weeping out into the street.

Should Tim have done what he did? No. He just yelled at a child for enjoying *The Phantom Menace* as a child. The movie was aimed at children. So the joke is on Tim, and is funny. Do I think adults should yell at children like that? Not normally no, but laughter at the situation does not mean approval. Often quite the opposite. The rules are different here because Tim, in *Spaced*, and the child are fictional characters.

Quite the character

So here's an extra level of complication with Adam's joke about Barbara to Colin. Adam might be a character in a sitcom with a reputation for making distasteful jokes or saying the unsayable, like David Brent from *The Office* – perhaps making a joke about Barbara's hair, Barbara also being in the sitcom. The whole thing is staged, including the hair. Does that make it okay? Daphne (remember Daphne?), also in the sitcom, might laugh. And Colin, the viewer at home, is amused that the scene was a disaster. He is laughing at the poor judgement of Adam. And that's the joke.

But the variables don't end there. Every joke is contending with the march of time, which affects our characters and contexts. We will look at that in the next chapter.

9

Leaping from car to car

I'm not a movie buff. I like comedies lasting 90 minutes that critics usually award three stars out of five. One of my all-time favourites is *Nuns on the Run*. I'm not making this up. It combines comedy and action with an ecclesiastical theme. And there's a car chase at the end. What's not to like?

Car chases are very important in action movies. More expensive Hollywood movies can afford to depict heroes fighting baddies on the tops of cars, trains and trucks. When they get desperate in sequels, they throw in helicopters. As the vehicles hurtle down the freeway towards a roadblock or a broken bridge, the characters leap from one vehicle on to another. One makes it. The other is sent tumbling to his or her death. Or a hand is outstretched and the preposterous drama continues.

It sounds extreme, but telling a joke is a bit like that: jumping from one moving car to another moving car via a third moving car.

Mood swings

We've already seen some of the parts that make up a joke. We've thought about Adam and Colin and the dizzying number of contexts for their joke about Barbara's hair, both real and fictional.

Being living, breathing, thinking, feeling beings, Adam, Barbara and Colin grow up, move on and change their minds and moods. They are not static. They are all moving, possibly at different speeds, which makes it complicated when information is being passed across.

The joke Adam decides to tell and the way he tells it depend on his mood at that exact moment. Maybe he went without breakfast, missed the bus and walked to work in the rain. The joke he might tell could be angry and mean-spirited. Poor Barbara is on the receiving end, and Colin is embarrassed.

Maybe Adam had an excellent breakfast, the bus arrived as he got to the stop, he got a seat, cheerfully surrendered it to a heavily pregnant woman, and now he arrives at work to find he's got a pay rise. All is well with the world and his joke is full of charm and playfulness.

Perhaps Colin didn't get a pay rise, even though his mortgage has gone up, and is simmering with rage and resentment. Barbara did get a pay rise and has just got her hair done, and jokes about her hair are fair game. Or maybe Barbara got fired, and Colin takes exception to Adam's joke, leaps to Barbara's defence and gets Adam disciplined, or even fired, for misogyny or racism.

Not only do moods change from day to day, but they change through seasons of life. An angry young woman may grow into a philosophical older women with an empty nest. They will find different things painfully funny, personally challenging and achingly twee. And their tastes within those phases may alter according to the weather, their medication and their relationships.

Films you thought were hilarious in your teens and watched again and again often seem just plain stupid when you revisit them 20 years later, when you are a slightly different person. The movie hasn't changed, but you have. (I'm pleased to say that I still find *Nuns on the Run* funny.)

New backdrops

In old Hanna–Barbera cartoons, backgrounds were recycled. The same wacky car passed a lot of cactuses that looked exactly the same. Real cars move around and the backdrop changes. It may be subtle, but over time a car on the open road will end up in suburbs and cities, and then out again into suburbs, plains, forests and mountains. Then it might pass through a tunnel, on to a transporter and then a ferry. It may be moving very slowly because of the traffic, or because it's been parked with the handbrake left off. One of those two scenarios is a disaster and could be expensive. It's also potentially funny.

Like the cars, Adam, Barbara and Colin are moving through different backdrops and contexts, where the customs and taboos are fluid. This is most obvious when watching comedy from decades earlier. Even if you think you haven't changed much, the spirit of the age has.

Watch an episode of *On the Buses* from the early 1970s and you will see attitudes of men towards women which nearly 50 years later seem, at best, very dated and, at worst, unpleasantly misogynistic. The writers of *On the Buses,* Ronald Chesney and Ronald Wolfe, were presenting fictional figures. They were not necessarily condoning their speech, although this does not, of course, give them a free pass. But they were writing in a particular time and making jokes they thought most people would find funny rather than distasteful.

Men behaving questionably

Sexual ethics and expectations have moved extremely quickly. Episodes of *Men Behaving Badly*, a popular mainstream show from the mid 1990s, now look, to some, rather questionable in terms of what is presented as funny and incongruous and what isn't.

In the 1970s and 1980s, male effeminacy provided gales of laughter in shows like *Are You Being Served?* These moments have a slightly different feel to them today in a culture which increasingly presents gender as fluid. The current feeling is that those who wish to change their gender should be understood rather than laughed at.

In the first series of *The League of Gentlemen* in 1999, a manly minicab driver was undergoing a sex change and went by the name of Barbara. The jokes were fairly straightforward and Barbara was seen as a figure of fun. When the BBC commissioned new TV episodes nearly 20 years later, it might have been easier to omit Barbara, but the show creators, to their credit, stuck to their guns and Barbara returned. This time, she had different jokes about gender pronouns and it seemed a better fit for the changed times.

Friends was a monster global sitcom hit that ran for ten years until 2004. When all 236 episodes of the show were uploaded to Netflix only 14 years later, news stories circulated that politically correct millennials found the show sexist, homophobic and transphobic. Comment pieces called millennials oversensitive, and the 24-hour news cycle was fed for another day.

When viewing comedies from yesteryear, the temptation is always to declare the protagonists, the writers, the producers and the guffawing audience bigots. But that just won't do. It fails to understand the context. And we should be careful lest history finds us wanting, as it surely will. Of what heinous sins will future generations be accusing us?

She's behind me, isn't she?

The context for a joke can change more rapidly still. Rather than in decades, things can change in seconds. The most obvious example is when you tell a joke about someone, thinking he can't hear you, only to realize he's just walked in and is standing behind you.

It can be funny to see that happen to someone, which is why it is a bit of a sitcom trope. I confess to writing (or at least co-writing) that joke twice. Once was in an episode of *Citizen Khan* in 2016 which was a fairly standard 'She's behind me, isn't she?' sort of joke. Three years earlier, in an episode of *Bluestone 42*, Richard Hurst and I wrote the same joke but with a twist. Bird, a robust and confrontational corporal, called Millsy a rude word. She realized that Millsy had walked in and was standing behind her. She said, 'He's behind me, isn't he?' before turning to Millsy and shamelessly saying the same rude word directly to his face.

41

What a difference a day makes

This sudden change to a context is normally situational. Prevailing social attitudes and taboos tend to change much more slowly over time. But sometimes they can be changed overnight if there is an event of sufficient seismic importance. Let us turn to one such event.

10

Comedy at Ground Zero

On 10 September 2001, the world was one way. On 12 September, it was another. Almost 3,000 people died when Al-Qaeda enacted their plan of mass destruction with 9/11. Some things that had been funny were no longer a joke a day or so later.

Nothing seemed funny at all for a while. Politics, culture and media had shifted. The mood had changed – although even that did not stay the same. Shock turned to rage, which morphed into revenge, followed by wars which brought about more death and destruction. Then came frustration and despair at intractable political military stalemates.

Too soon

The writer of Ecclesiastes, found in the Wisdom books of the Old Testament, writes about this change in mood in chapter 3, verse 4: there is 'a time to weep, and a time to laugh; a time to mourn, and a time to dance'. The aftermath of 9/11 was not a time for jokes. Can 'the line' that the media are so desperate to draw be found somewhere around Ground Zero?

No one was in the mood to laugh on 12 September. It didn't stay that way, of course. But the time to laugh arrived sooner than one might have thought. *The Onion*, an online spoof newspaper, was among the first to offer up some jokes a couple of weeks later. Their 26 September issue was entitled 'Holy Fucking Shit: Attack on America', featuring articles with headlines like: 'Not Knowing

What Else To Do, Woman Bakes American Flag Cake' and 'U.S. Vows To Defeat Whoever It Is We're At War With'. Skilled writers found a way to make the toxic and taboo not only funny but cathartic. Slowly, with jokes, the USA recovered.

Searching for the line

It turns out 'the line' can't even be drawn around Ground Zero where thousands perished. But what about the Second World War death camps, where millions perished? Is the Holocaust off limits? The extermination of millions of Jews, or anything close to it, is surely no laughing matter? Not quite so.

Ask Roberto Benigni, who co-wrote, directed and starred in *Life is Beautiful*. Given its subject matter of Italian concentration camps, it was understandably controversial, not least because it was comic in tone.

Many were offended by it. One critic, surprisingly, was Mel Brooks, writer and director of *The Producers*. He said Benigni had no right to make the film, being a Gentile and therefore personally unaffected by the reality of the Holocaust. But surely Gentiles are capable of feeling the astonishing tragedy of such a terrible event?

Arguments can be made either way, but it should also be noted the movie proved commercially and critically successful. This in itself does not make it okay. Pornographic movies are often successful and are fully appreciated by their audience. Customer satisfaction does not necessarily confer moral acceptability.

It was clear from the movie that Benigni was not intending to make light of Jewish suffering in Italy, at least. Some may have found the movie too distressing to watch, but that is not the same as saying he had no right to make the movie or should have been prevented from doing so.

It's all different now

As we reach the end of Part 1, however, we have seen that the issues surrounding comedy and jokes are more fraught than ever.

The gatekeepers of the media have been overpowered, the gates torn down and the keys thrown into the river. Making and releasing a movie like *Life is Beautiful* took millions of pounds and access to a distributor. Writing a controversial column in a newspaper couldn't be done without an editor and a publisher putting on the brakes. Such a world was easy to regulate. Publishers could be sued or be forced to print retractions or apologies. Controversial movies were made and released with certificates to warn the public about content. The makers of *The Life of Brian* and *The Last Temptation of Christ* knew exactly what they were doing and where they stood legally.

Today's media landscape is very different. Anyone can be a journalist, publisher, film-maker, comedian or columnist. You just need a smart phone. A video can be uploaded to YouTube and become a news story within hours, especially if you're a public figure. But even so-called private citizens can find themselves in a media storm when someone finds a video or tweet that was posted and decides to take offence and blow the whistle. We saw this with the Tweet by Paul Chambers about Robin Hood Airport and Mark Meechan's 'Nazi Saluting Pug Dog' YouTube video. We will look at the latter in more detail in Part 3.

Lawmakers and politicians have struggled to catch up with the realities of the always-on unfiltered media. But even carefully considered, well-drafted laws will not prevent the news cycle throwing up stories of jokes causing grave offence, howls of protest and battle lines being drawn.

Blessed are the peacemakers

In this context, the Church could have a role to play. After all, a divine being once said, 'Blessed are the peacemakers' (or 'cheesemakers', depending on how far back you were standing at the Sermon on the Mount, according to Monty Python's *Life of Brian*). The Church would love to see herself as a healer of divisions and a forum in which warring factions can be brought together and reconciled.

Sadly, this is not where the Church has historically been strong. For centuries, she has demonstrated a distant and dysfunctional relationship with comedy. Christians have more often been part of the problem, rather than part of the solution.

In the next part of this book, we will see why that has been the case, and why there is much more evidence for a divine sense of humour than one might think.

Part 2

COMEDY AND THE CHURCH

11

Do Christians have a sense of humour?

I t is often said that the devil has all the best tunes. But does he also have all the best jokes? If you watch a musical, the hero or heroine's songs will be idealistic and emotional, lyrical and beautiful. But not funny.

In *West Side Story*, Tony sings a song about the girl he has just met, called Maria. In *Jesus Christ Superstar*, Mary Magdalene sings that she doesn't know how to love Jesus. Both songs are beautiful. But neither is funny.

There is usually an overtly comic song in every musical. In *West Side Story*, the funny song is about transgressive hoodlums impersonating a policeman called Officer Krupke. They are essentially shaking their fists against the institutions and adults in their lives that have let them down. In *Jesus Christ Superstar*, the funniest song belongs to feckless collaborator King Herod. He patronizes Jesus and makes wisecracks about his miracles. In the filmed production of the musical in 2000, Herod was played by comedian Rik Mayall.

Jesus Christ Superstar is not seeking to poke fun at the story of Jesus Christ. Lloyd Webber and Rice take the story seriously and are broadly faithful to it.[1] The show is a rock opera, not a comedy. While there is playful language and humour used throughout the show, it is significant that the most classically comic song is

---

[1] The omission of Jesus' resurrection at the end seems curious, given how faithful the show is to the Christian story.

Herod's humiliation of Jesus. Does comedy seem to be a tactic of the devil? Is that why the Church is uneasy when it comes to jokes?

The gospel according to sitcom

Although comedy is often seen as worryingly subversive, there are plenty of examples of affectionate ecclesiastical comedies that didn't seem to upset anyone. Derek Nimmo made a career out of playing inoffensive monks and priests in sitcoms including *All Gas and Gaiters* (1966–71), *Oh, Brother!* (1968–70) and *Hell's Bells* (1986).

More recently, *The Vicar of Dibley* has shown the humorous goings-on in a Church of England parish through the eyes of a female priest, Geraldine. There were only 20 episodes between 1994 and 2007, but they have been repeated many times. The series came third in a nationwide poll for Britain's Best Sitcom in 2004. Since then, *Rev*, a comedy about the depressing life of an urban vicar, Adam Smallbone, has run for three series and won a Bafta for Best Sitcom in 2011.[2] In all of these shows, people of faith, especially clergy, have been taken seriously and portrayed sympathetically.

The Festival of Light

The broader picture is more mixed. The man in the street, or the lady in the pew, may have been broadly happy with the representation of Christianity in popular culture over the past few decades, but others have not. The shining example here is the Festival of Light movement, led by Mary Whitehouse. She objected loudly and stridently to numerous cultural depictions of the Christian story, including works such *The Life of Brian, The Last Temptation*

---

[2] For more examples, see Bryony Taylor's delightful *More TV, Vicar? Christians on the Telly: The Good, the Bad and the Quirky* (London: Darton, Longman and Todd, 2016).

of Christ and a poem published in *Gay News* called 'The Love that Dares to Speak Its Name'.

Whitehouse was not merely concerned for the representation of Christianity in the media, she was concerned about public standards more widely. She was hardly a voice in the wilderness, finding allies in Cliff Richard and Malcolm Muggeridge. Her Nationwide Petition for Public Decency in 1972 garnered over 1.3 million signatures.[3]

As you would expect, or may indeed remember, she was also regularly mocked for holding broadcasters to account. She was derided for counting the swearwords in TV shows, which she did for sitcoms like *Till Death Us Do Part*. The pornographic magazine *Whitehouse* was ironically named after her, as was the BBC comedy *The Mary Whitehouse Experience*, which launched Rob Newman, David Baddiel, Steve Punt and Hugh Dennis.

Public figures continue to speak up in the same way. Later in Part 2, we shall see that Ann Widdecombe, publicly known as a devout Roman Catholic, has argued that modern comedy is often too blasphemous. Promoting a BBC TV documentary in the *Daily Telegraph*, she wrote, 'Gentle mockery or sharp satire aimed at Christians and their leaders have been replaced by abuse of Christianity itself.'[4]

Others, however, cringe when Christians speak up in such a way, fearing it makes Christianity look rather sour. Our culture places great importance on being able to take a joke, and some feel that appearing to have a sense of humour failure makes Christianity less attractive.

---

[3] Dominic Sandbrook, *State of Emergency, The Way We Were: Britain 1970–74* (London: Allen Lane, 2010), p. 462.

[4] 'Christians are the Butt of Bad Jokes', *Daily Telegraph*, 27 March 2013: <www.telegraph.co.uk/lifestyle/9957059/Ann-Widdecombe-Christians-are-the-butt-of-bad-jokes.html>.

The mystery of comedy

The Church is not without its comic traditions. Medieval mystery plays performed on feast days would often contain humour. Dr Hetta Elizabeth Howes, lecturer in Medieval and Early Modern Literature at City, University of London, writes,

> Students of medieval mystery plays are often surprised, even shocked, by their humour. Noah is portrayed as a bit of a drunken fool, and his wife as a shrewish nag. The York play of the Crucifixion, which concerns Jesus being nailed to the Cross, sees the soldiers arguing and making the audience laugh with their incompetence.[5]

The idea that Noah was a drunken fool has biblical underpinnings. Read Genesis chapter 9 and you will find the great Noah embarrassingly drunk and naked. This is both comic and tragic, not least because he is leader of the new human race after the great flood, and he's got drunk and exposed himself. *Plus ça change.*

As we continue with Part 2 of this book, we will see many examples of how the Bible is far more transgressive and bawdy than modern-day Christians might like to admit. Medieval Christians, however, seemed to have no problem with this fact and built it into their stories and feast day performances, which were designed to make the crowds laugh as well as gasp and cheer.

In Part 3, we will also see how Easter used to be a time for preachers to tell jokes. These theatrical and comic traditions declined with the Reformation in the sixteenth century, which emphasized the preaching of the Bible and a call to personal holiness. As a rule, reformers frowned on drama and iconography.

In the following decades, the spirit of the Reformation continued with Puritans like Oliver Cromwell. When he became

---

[5] <www.bl.uk/medieval-literature/articles/medieval-drama-and-the-mystery-plays>.

Lord Protector of the Commonwealth, he closed all the theatres in England. This speaks of an attitude that does not have much use for light entertainment.

Burning zeal

Fiction often provides neat summaries of particular mindsets. This over-zealous attitude to policing jokes is beautifully personified in Umberto Eco's brilliant debut novel, *The Name of the Rose*. Jorge, an austere monk, tells Franciscan friar William of Baskerville (played by Sean Connery in the movie) that laughter comes from the devil and removes fear. And without fear there cannot be faith. Comedy is no laughing matter as the souls of millions are at stake. It drives Jorge to take extreme action.

Eco's novel is set in 1327 and was written in 1980. Is Jorge more of a modern-day prude than a realistically zealous monk? Either way, the character of Jorge has a resonance which makes him a believable type. Critics of Mary Whitehouse might find Jorge's sense of humour failure very convincing and a legitimate portrayal of the Church's attitude to jokes.

Reviving the tradition

More recently, Christians and church groups have sought to embrace the culture and reclaim a theatrical tradition, using comedy to explain theology and biblical themes. The Riding Lights Theatre Company, based in York, home of the famous cycle of mystery plays, has been doing just that for 40 years. Like a number of other companies, they tour the nation's churches, schools and theatres with shows that aim to make people laugh as well as think.

What we see, then, is a confusing picture of Christians who embrace the culture of comedy and those who remain deeply suspicious of it. The problem is it's not a fair fight. Attacking jokes and blowing the whistle is much easier than defending jokes. We can see this in the Chambers Twitter case. Advocates of free speech were forced to defend a threat to an airport. For defenders of Count Dankula and his Nazi-saluting dog, it was even more painful. Defenders of free speech often find themselves on the side of people they do not like or would rather not speak up for.

Moreover, it is always possible to make a case against jokes, citing them as 'dangerous' or 'damaging', highlighting the plight of victims. This happens regularly in our always-on, hyperbolic Western culture in which Twitter mobs leap on a phrase or word used by someone who might not even be in the public eye to show how people could have been hurt or offended by such terminology.[6] This becomes a news story which then escalates until 48 hours later, when a fresh linguistic scandal arrives to provide new talking points. Individuals are left to pick up the pieces.

If the Church wishes to be a peacemaker or to reclaim any credible reputation for being able to take a joke, she must resist the urge to be drawn into stoking the fires of this perpetual outrage machine. She must think carefully about comedy, not least because her very foundational document, the Bible, portrays the founder, Jesus Christ, as funny. This is not how Jesus is regularly shown dramatically or artistically. But what is the reason for this disconnection?

---

[6] Examples abound, especially in Jon Ronson's *So You've Been Publicly Shamed* (New York: Riverhead, 2015).

12

The problem with jokes

Let me share with you a regular occurrence in my life as a comedy writer. I shall do so in script form.

INT. OFFICE. DAY

James Cary is sitting in a production office with a producer who is trying to produce a cheap online advert for a high-street bank. He has just shown James Cary some funny online adverts by small start-up companies, promoting photo albums and smoothies respectively.

PRODUCER: So the client wants to do an online advert like those ones. Something low budget and funny.

JAMES: No, no. They don't want something funny.

PRODUCER: They do.

JAMES: Yes, they *say* they do, but they really don't. The moment banks see jokes they panic.

PRODUCER: That can happen, sure, but they say they're not going to do that. They're serious.

JAMES: That's what I'm worried about. Banks are very serious.

PRODUCER: Honestly. It'll be fine. They want to do something funny.

JAMES: Big banks love the idea of comedy, and their marketing people can all remember those adverts for Tango and Carling Black Label back in the day. But the moment they see something with jokes in it and their logo on it, they fuss and worry and want to take off all the edges, to the point where it's not funny. And it's not drama either. It's just bland people talking about mortgages or financial products.

PRODUCER: Okay, I'll bear that in mind. But here's the brief.

Producer explains the situation and, a few days later, James provides a script with jokes in.

CUT to one week later. Producer phones James. Split screen.

PRODUCER: Love the script. And I showed it to the bank and they loved it too. Really loved it. But they are a bit worried about the tone. And some of the jokes. They're sending it to Legal to check it's okay.

JAMES: Ha ha. Because no one understands jokes better than a lawyer, right?

PRODUCER: Ha. Yeah. But they really want to do this. They really like the idea but just want to 'check in' on some of the jokes. But basically, I think we'll be fine.

JAMES: Trust me. We won't be. But let me know.

CUT to two weeks later. James at his desk receives a call from the producer. Split screen.

PRODUCER: Yeah, really sorry, but they decided to go a different way on this one . . .

JAMES: *(Trying to sound surprised)* Really?

PRODUCER: Yeah. They passed it around and felt they might be implying that some of their customers were stupid. Or that some of their employees were stupid. Or that –

JAMES: It's okay. I get it. It happens all the time. I still get
            paid, right?

PRODUCER: Yeah, of course! They're a bank. Money's not a prob-
            lem.

JAMES: Great. I'll invoice you. Bye.

The above scenario has happened to me with banks at least three
times. I mention it because this typical story highlights that large
institutions are extremely risk averse. You might think that the
larger an institution, the greater its global reach, the more solid its
foundations, the braver it could be.

That's not how it works. Large corporations feel they have
much more to lose. And employees of that company don't want
to be the ones who start the rot. It's always easier to avoid jokes.

Corporate joke aversion

This is not, of course, limited to banks. All kinds of corporations
and institutions have CJA (Corporate Joke Aversion). It partly
explains why commercial radio stations are often accused of
being bland. A friend of mine, who must remain nameless, works
for a major commercial music radio station and, despite being a
comedian, is regularly asked by management to make fewer jokes.
Why? Because a joke that goes wrong may offend a listener, cause
a network sponsor to pull out and cost the station thousands of
pounds in lost advertising revenue. Is any joke ever worth that?

Large institutions like to be in control of everything. And jokes
are fundamentally anarchic. No matter what safeguards and rules
you put in place, jokes wear clever disguises, dig tunnels and imp-
ishly creep through the defences. Therefore, it's just easier and
safer to avoid jokes altogether. Give in to CJA.

Plausible deniability

I also experienced CJA first hand, when co-writing my TV sitcom
set in an army bomb disposal unit in Afghanistan, *Bluestone 42*.

The programme was made by the BBC, a large, risk-averse institution under constant scrutiny from the press and the government. Auntie Beeb is very careful and likes to control and manage everything, leaving nothing to chance.

Our attempts to get the Ministry of Defence to co-operate with the show in providing advice, access or equipment were entirely in vain. The MOD has a bad case of CJA and is every bit as cautious and controlling as the BBC. When it was clear that the MOD would have no creative or editorial control, very little assistance was forthcoming. This meant that if jokes were broadcast that were deemed in poor taste, reflecting badly on Her Majesty's Armed Forces, the Ministry of Defence could deny all responsibility. They have a name and reputation to protect and maintain.

Under pressure

Church leaders also feel CJA. They are motivated by concern for the good name of their denomination, be it Roman Catholic, Anglican or Southern Baptist. But there is an even greater burden. They rightly feel concern for the good name of Jesus Christ. Why risk harming the name of Christ and the Church over something as trivial as a joke? It just isn't worth it.

Some church leaders are more relaxed about this than others. The likes of the Revd Richard Coles are adept at holding their own on a satirical BBC panel show like *Have I Got News For You?* Other church leaders would find this very difficult or profoundly dangerous. Of course, the most cautious attitude can be found in our fictional friend Jorge in *The Name of the Rose*. He is obviously an extreme case, but everyone has to work out where they feel jokes are unhelpful or chaotically dangerous.

Jokes have a habit of creating unintended consequences, especially when churches try to be even slightly funny, light-hearted and self-deprecating. It can easily go wrong. Publications like

The problem with jokes

Reader's Digest[1] and social media are awash with examples of witty church signs that turn out to have unfortunate double meanings or associations. Like 'Now is a great time to visit! (Our Pastor is on vacation)' or 'How to have a better marriage every Thursday at 6.30 p.m.' Some Googling will find you many more examples that are unintentionally very rude indeed. Let the Googler beware.

The biggest challenge of all

Churches have even more to worry about than their reputation in their home town, the image of the wider denomination and the good name of Jesus Christ. They have to worry about fellow Christians, many of whom have strong views on what is and is not funny or appropriate. Many do not shrink from offering such opinions, thinking they have the Bible on their side.

---

[1] <www.rd.com/funny-stuff/funny-church-signs/>.

13

The Philippians 4 manoeuvre

But sexual immorality and all impurity or covetousness must
not even be named among you, as is proper among saints.
Let there be no filthiness nor foolish talk nor crude joking,
which are out of place, but instead let there be thanksgiving.
(Ephesians 5.3–4)

This passage of Scripture is not a promising manifesto for making jokes. Lots of jokes revel in obscenity, foolishness and coarseness, perhaps the vast majority in the realm of stand-up comedy and jokes told in the pub after work. The Bible says this way of talking is out of place among those who call themselves Christians. Does this put comedy off limits for the Church? Was Mary Whitehouse right all along?

Christians need to take this, and every, passage of the Bible seriously. But we should also note that Paul is being specific. He is writing about the personal conduct of Christians and the standard to which they should hold themselves. Christians really should think carefully about the jokes they tell and the words they use.

But most of the comedy we see on screens is depictions of characters who do not hold themselves to a biblical standard, even on the rare occasions these characters are written by Christians. I found myself explaining this when my aforementioned TV show, *Bluestone 42*, was broadcast on BBC3. Some Christians found it troubling that a fellow Christian had written a sitcom in which most of the characters swear liberally and with feeling. They swear literally like troopers. They tell one another to get stuffed in all manner of inventively obscene and abrupt ways. How is that okay?

Discerning voices

I'm not a character in *Bluestone 42*. You will note that I'm not using the expletives from the show in this book, and not even quoting them. I have preferred to used euphemisms like 'tell one another to get stuffed in all manner of ways' to convey the kinds of words that were used in *Bluestone 42*. I feel an obligation to do that because, as a Christian, Paul's words of Ephesians 5.4 apply to me, unlike all but one of the characters in *Bluestone 42*. I am writing this book in my own voice so I must take heed of Ephesians 5.

I also want to tell the truth. In fact, I want to be doubly truthful. As a Christian, I want to be truthful. As a comedy writer, I know that comedy is based on truth, so if I want to be funny I have to tell the truth. Scrubbing bad language from a military situation diminishes the honesty of the story and undermines the comedy. If a bomb detonates near a soldier, he does not exclaim 'Oh dear!' or 'Good heavens!' When a sergeant barks orders under attack, he or she speaks with great emphasis and uses very salty language (and not the kind of salty language to which the Apostle Paul refers in Colossians 4.6). To portray the soldiers exclaiming 'Fiddlesticks!' when they're being hit in the chest by a rocket-propelled grenade would be dishonest and silly.

Incidentally, an exception to this rule would be subverting the expectation of bad language for comedy purposes. It would be an incongruous and funny moment if you were expecting to hear cussing but heard only the mildest of expletives. In fact, Captain Nick Medhurst, played by Oliver Chris in *Bluestone 42*, often says, 'Oh dear.' During one particularly vicious battle in Series 3,

Episode 1, he also pokes his head out of an armoured vehicle and says, 'Everything all right, loves?' The incongruity is funny, but you can't do it all the time for every character.

Characters in comedies do and say things all the time that their creators do not agree with. Johnny Speight, the writer of *Till Death Us Do Part* (which became *All in the Family* in the USA) did not condone the racist words of Alf Garnett (or Archie Bunker in the USA). To Speight, the words he put into the mouth of Alf Garnett were so self-evidently absurd and wrong that they were funny, although the audience did not always agree on why they were funny.

Sitcom heroes and heroines are deeply flawed people doing foolish things for mixed motives, normally operating within some kind of Judeo-Christian moral framework. People make this mistake when they quote Shakespeare, as if he personally was writing down truths about life for all people in all times and all places. Some phrases have that quality to them, but these *bons mots* were sections of speeches said by characters in their own given fictional or quasi-historical situation. We should be rather cautious about taking life advice from Danish princes or Scottish kings.

The Philippians 4 manoeuvre

Ephesians 5 is not the only text in the Bible that can be quoted by modern-day Jorges. They could try and pull something that I call the 'Philippians 4 manoeuvre'. If you really want a proof text to criticize anything you consider to be filthy or wrong, quote Paul's words from his letter to the Philippians:

> Finally, brothers, whatever is true, whatever is honourable, whatever is just, whatever is pure, whatever is lovely, whatever is commendable, if there is any excellence, if there is anything worthy of praise, think about these things.
>
> (Philippians 4.8)

Good news stories

The verse is delightful, but is it helpful? Again, we need to take these inspired words seriously. But are Christians required to apply them to *all* situations? In 1993, BBC News presenter Martyn Lewis spoke out against to the continual diet of bad news stories. He questioned the choice of newsrooms perpetuating an agenda that relentlessly highlighted disasters and tragedies.[1]

Those who remember Lewis's comments may also recall Trevor MacDonald's contribution to this debate with his 'And finally' stories at the end of the ITN news bulletins. They were normally upbeat, quirky or sentimental items which offered a shift in tone from the rest of the programme.[2] Is this a Christian approach?

We should be careful about assuming that Christians should filter out bad news, or remove characters from comedies because they are not honourable, pure and lovely. Removing such characters would mean hardly a single situation comedy would survive. Perhaps the cast of *Dad's Army* might make it, but there would be no Basil Fawlty, Victor Meldrew or Edina and Patsy.

The whole story

If we read the Bible from beginning to end, we see a far more nuanced picture. The verse in Philippians also becomes all the more striking because the Bible contains so many stories of people who were dishonourable, impure and vile.

The Bible is littered with stories of liars, tyrants, prostitutes, murderers and adulterers. And those are the good guys. The great prophet Moses was a killer and a coward. The forerunner of Christ, King David, was an adulterer and a murderer. Rahab

---

[1] <www.independent.co.uk/voices/not-my-idea-of-good-news-at-the-end-of-a-week-of-horrifying-events-martyn-lewis-bbc-presenter-argues-1457539.html>.

[2] Sometimes this shift in tone was very awkward. Such moments were parodied extremely well in BBC TV's spoof-news comedy *The Day Today*.

was a prostitute, Noah a drunk, Jacob a fraudster, Peter a coward and Paul a Christian-killer, to say nothing of Samson, Solomon and so many others.

The only exception we find is Jesus, who was none of these things. When the Monty Python team set out to write *The Life of Brian* the target was originally going to be Jesus, but they found his life to be beyond reproach. But even Jesus told stories of treachery, violence and envy. In a parable recorded in Matthew 21.33–41, we read a story in which tenants seize a vineyard, beat and kill servants and then kill the vineyard owner's own son. Elsewhere we read that a man is attacked, robbed and left for dead and ignored by hypocrites before a Good Samaritan comes along. The brother of the Prodigal Son is cold-hearted and resentful.

The Bible is not an easy read and does not come with a 'U' certificate. One hesitates before reading it to children, or even adults. There are many stories which involve bodily functions and words we would rather not hear read out loud in church. But do we find rude words in our Bibles? Modern translators seem to be rather prudish on that score. We need to lift the lid on biblical toilet humour.

14

Holy crap!

Let's face it. The title of this chapter could be a lot worse. Some readers may be appalled at the title as it leaps off the page. Am I being unchristian for using such words so brazenly? Does the fact that I'm using such a word to make a point mean it is artistically justified? Is 'artistically justified' even a legitimate defence? Maybe. But is it biblically justified?

The Bible does not shy away from stories of drunkards and prostitutes. Nor do the Bible writers shy away from using words that would make a congregation blush.

But our attitudes to those words are not necessarily biblical. Churches are only rarely embarrassed on Sunday mornings because of our modern translations. We think our ancestors were prudish, but a brief look at older versions of the Bible will reveal that the opposite is true.

The King James Version (KJV) of the Bible was published in 1611. It has been heavily romanticized as containing beautiful English, helping to define the language itself.[1] But this linguistic and cultural gem does not shy away from the original Greek and Hebrew texts. For example, in the Old Testament, you will find an expression about men who are described as 'those that piss against the wall' (KJV). Lovers of the King James Version tend not

---

[1] It was only many years after the King James Version was published that it was heralded as a marvel of the English language. For more on this, see Alister McGrath, *In the Beginning: The Story of the King James Bible and How It Changed a Nation, a Language, and a Culture* (Harlow: Anchor, 2002).

to mention that expression, even though it occurs six times in that translation.

Today's congregations are spared this particular embarrassment of having such words read out in church on a Sunday morning because most modern translations of the Bible omit them. Instead, they render that expression simply as 'men' or 'males'. The urine has evaporated without a trace.[2]

Bible translators could argue that in those six cases the sense of the original Hebrew was not seeking to highlight bodily emissions, but merely highlight the maleness of the people in question. But if we read other stories in the Bible, we will see scatological stories, some of which are grimly amusing.

Toilet humour

Turn to Judges chapter 3 and, once you've sneaked past the wonderfully named Mesopotamian king Chushan-rishathaim, whose name means Double Bad Cushite King, you will find a Moabite king named Eglon who enslaved the Israelites for 18 years. Eventually, the Israelites cried out for deliverance, as they do in Judges quite often, with almost comic regularity. A man named Ehud was raised up to assassinate Eglon with a long, two-edged dagger hidden by his thigh (Judges 3.16).[3] Eglon was so fat that when Ehud took his chance to be alone with the king and stab him, the entire dagger disappeared into Eglon's body.

But the narrative does not stop with the slaying of the Bible's answer to Jabba the Hutt. The dagger caused a rupture of King Eglon's bowels. This stank so badly that the embarrassed guards decided against interrupting the king, assuming he was catching up with some light reading on the toilet. On this occasion, a euphemism is employed in the Hebrew which translates as 'covering his feet' but the image is very clear. The moment is humorous,

---

[2] Could we say that Bible translators have been literally taking the piss? Discuss.
[3] Judges 3.16 is far more intriguing than John 3.16.

not least because the hesitation and embarrassment enabled Ehud to make his escape. This is not a reading you tend to get on Sunday mornings in church.

Rubbish translations

In the New Testament, in Philippians 3.8, the Apostle Paul writes about how wonderful it is to know Christ and how everything else, in comparison, is 'rubbish'. He does not hold back in his metaphor, using a Greek word that does not appear anywhere else in the New Testament. It's the word *skubala*. The English Standard Version renders the word 'rubbish', while the earthier King James Version renders that word more correctly as 'dung'. The latter is far closer to the true meaning, which is much more excremental.

Paul has some form in this area, creating powerfully disturbing images in his letters. In his letter to the Galatians, he heavily criticizes a group of Jews who were insisting that Gentiles had to become Jews in order to become Christians. This involved circumcising grown men. Paul said this procedure was no longer necessary and said that he wished that those who continued to enforce this practice would, according to the Good News Bible translation, 'go all the way' and 'castrate themselves' (Galatians 5.12).

Is this kind of language praiseworthy or lovely? No. But it is necessary. And comic. And biblical. Are Christians showing themselves to be more prudish than the actual words of the Bible? Are we in danger of making the mistake of the Pharisees who considered themselves to be holier than Jesus?

15

No laughing Messiah

In 1999, the Churches Advertising Network enjoyed some success in the UK by depicting Jesus Christ as a type of revolutionary. A picture of Jesus reminiscent of an iconic image of Che Guevara was put above the strapline 'Meek. Mild. As if.'[1] The association had resonance because we have no trouble imagining Jesus being angry. An account of Jesus turning over tables in the Temple courts occurs in all four Gospels. John (2.15) tells us that Jesus even made a whip.

Jesus was clearly capable of anger, but also of grief. 'Jesus wept' is not only a popular blasphemy but a compelling image, again from John's Gospel. It takes place when Jesus is informed of his friend Lazarus's death (John 11.35). We see anger and tears. But no laughter on the part of Jesus. Why not?

In *The Name of the Rose*, William (Sean Connery, remember?) says that monkeys do not laugh, and that laughter is particular to humanity. Jorge ripostes that sin is also particular to humanity and that, just as Christ did not sin, so he never laughed. Jorge is implying that laughter is beneath Jesus and inherently sinful. Is Jorge correct? Did Christ not laugh?

In one sense, yes! There is no verse in the Bible that says 'Jesus laughed.' But is the idea of Jesus tipping back his head and laughing heartily unthinkable? Jesus and his 12 disciples spent months together on the road. There must have been teasing, mocking

---

[1] <http://churchads.net/our-campaigns/meek-mild-as-if/>.

and in-jokes. At times, they must surely have got the giggles and ended up rolling around on the floor laughing. Perhaps. If they did, the Gospel writers did not record those bits. And there are no extended versions of the Gospels available with previously unseen footage. If there were, I suspect those bits would contain much laughter and merriment (like most blooper reels). But this is conjecture.

Jesus in art

Two thousand years of Christian art has given us an enduring image of a serious Christ. Whether he is rendered in stained glass in a church or painted by an Old Master as a pallid northern European, Jesus' expression is usually stern. If not stern, then thoughtful, wistful or sad. But never amused, smirking or grinning at Peter getting it wrong again.

In the movies, Jesus is similarly mirthless. For many people of a certain age,[2] Jesus *is* Robert Powell, who played the eponymous role in *Jesus of Nazareth* with great intensity. Subsequent portrayals have been no less serious. In the global box office smash *The Passion of the Christ*, Jesus was not big on laughing. The Jesus seen in the musical *Godspell* is more light-hearted, but this is a notable exception.

There are less reverent versions of Jesus, such as those in the long-running animation *South Park* and the stage show *Jerry Springer: The Opera*, but these come from outside the church tradition and are intentionally subversive. In fact, they comically depend on the fact that Jesus is typically considered to be an august and humourless figure.

Even G. K. Chesterton, who was well known for seeing the humorous paradox in everything, concurred with this seriousness of Jesus when he wrote: 'There was one thing that was too great for God to show us when He walked upon our earth; and I

---

[2] Like my mother, for example.

have sometimes fancied that it was His mirth.'[3] Is this true? Did Jesus keep his sense of humour to himself?

While I would not argue that Jesus was a comedian, he does clearly make use of comedy and satire. We will examine that in due course, but first let us consider who Jesus is, and how his dual nature as God and Man is already intrinsically funny.

16

The Supreme Being walks into a bar . . .

I can still remember the first time I saw the 1978 *Superman* film. It was on television in the early 1980s. One line has remained lodged in my memory ever since. Superman catches Lois Lane as she drops from a tall building. 'I've got you,' he says, with a reassuring smile. Lane instinctively sums up the comedy of being rescued by a flying superhero. Seeing Superman is hovering in mid-air, she says, 'You've got me? Who's got you?!' An excellent question.

Lois was reacting like someone who had never seen a flying superhero before. We need to remember this reaction as we read about the disciples, the Pharisees and the crowds encountering Christ for the first time 2,000 years ago.

Remember also that Superman was originally a character from a comic. Most superheroes come from comic books. In the past 20 years, superhero films have become expensive, dark, brooding and self-important. But superheroes are funny because, while they look like ordinary people (except for the Spandex suit and pants on the outside), they have secret, special and surprising superpowers. There is great comic incongruity.

Countless articles have been written about the fact that Superman and most superheroes are essentially Christ figures. They normally have to sacrifice themselves or make themselves vulnerable in some way in order to save the world from evil. What is often forgotten is the very incongruity of the superhero and the Christ figure. The notion that God becomes a man is funny. It is so comically absurd that Islam rejects Christianity almost entirely on this basis: a Trinitarian deity, one Person of whom becomes human. To them, it's blasphemous, illogical and laughable.

I don't believe it

We see a similar reaction in the Gospel accounts. Those around Jesus scoffed at the idea that this human carpenter could have cosmic powers. At the beginning of Mark's Gospel, Jesus forgives the sin of a paralysed man and the scribes consider this blasphemy (2.7). How can a mere man forgive sins? Only God can do that, they mutter to one another. It had not occurred to them that this man, or indeed any man, could be God. Jesus, with his super-hearing, knew what they were saying, and interrupted and challenged them. Then he showed his super-healing by inviting the paralysed man to get up and walk. Note the reaction in Mark 2.12: 'They were all amazed and glorified God, saying, "We never saw anything like this!"' It was true. They hadn't.

Throughout the Gospels, the divinity of Christ and the humility of his birthplace and status cause regular stupefaction and scandal, often with comic results. We see an example in the first chapter of John's Gospel. Philip found Nathanael and excitedly said to him: '"We have found him of whom Moses in the Law and also the prophets wrote, Jesus of Nazareth, the son of Joseph!" Nathanael said to him, "Can anything good come out of Nazareth?"' (John 1.45–46).

Boom. Funny. That's Philip told. Nathanael's line is reminiscent of Lady Bracknell's line in *The Importance of Being Earnest*: 'A handbag?' She is responding to Earnest's revelation of his situation when he was found as a baby in the cloakroom of Victoria Station.

Further enquiry from Nathanael would have revealed that Jesus was placed in a manger on his birth. An animal feeding trough! How could this low-born human be God Incarnate?

Blindingly funny

It was not just Jesus' identity and birthplace that produced shocks and scandal. Thanks to his divinity, Jesus was able to display astonishing power to heal the sick, give sight to the blind and even raise the dead. Reactions to these moments and the utter befuddlement of Jesus' onlookers are often comic.

We see such a reaction in an event known as the Transfiguration that is found in Matthew, Mark and Luke's Gospels. Peter, James and John witness Jesus speaking to Moses and Elijah. Moses had died centuries earlier in the desert, and Elijah was last seen being carried up to heaven by a whirlwind.

This would be like accompanying the current monarch of England into a secret chamber beneath Trafalgar Square and watching her speak to Alfred the Great and Henry V. It's so incongruous and stupefying that it's funny. In a movie, such a scene would almost certainly be played for laughs.[1] In his Gospel, Mark nods to the strangeness of this event when he tells us that Peter, on seeing Elijah and Moses, offers to put up three tents because 'He did not know what to say, for they were terrified' (9.6).

Peter was often quick to speak while still processing how Jesus' divinity worked. Reading the Gospels through, you could argue that he appears to be a Homer Simpson type, getting the wrong end of the stick most of the time and having to learn the hard way. It is very endearing, and many of us could identify with the way that Peter instinctively reacts.

We see such a reaction in the chapter of Mark's Gospel before the Transfiguration, when Peter heard that Jesus must be rejected and killed. Peter took Jesus aside to rebuke him (Mark 8.32), to

---

[1] It is reminiscent of the scene in *Indiana Jones and the Last Crusade* when Indy meets a knight from the First Crusade who is nearly 1,000 years old. As you might expect, some of this is played for laughs. The ancient knight is comically unable to wield his sword, and there's a lovely joke when businessman Walter Donovan drinks from the wrong grail, ages supernaturally quickly and explodes.

which Jesus famously replied, 'Get behind me, Satan!' Poor Peter. He really was trying his best. How was he supposed to react to such an extraordinary God–man?

I'd like to make a complaint

But we also see hostile reactions and some kind of cognitive dissonance from Jesus' enemies. In chapter 9 of John's Gospel, Jesus gives sight to a man born blind. You might expect to see universal joy and celebration at such a display of benign power. Instead, we see rage and indignation, not least because Jesus has done this awful thing on the Sabbath. How could he do such a wicked thing?

The ex-blind man is questioned by the Pharisees. Then his parents are called for and questioned about whether he was even blind in the first place. At one point, the guileless former blind man wonders if these scribes' obsession with Jesus is because they just want to become disciples too (9.27). They do not. And they get very angry. And it's funny.

Double take

There is a standard trope in action movies when something extra-ordinary happens. A lone witness, often a security guard or home-less person on a park bench, double-takes at the strange sight, then checks the drink in his or her hand. Clearly, what the witness just saw was a hallucination caused by unexpectedly strong alcohol.[2]

Jesus' ministry on earth is full of moments that could provoke such a reaction. The sight of Jesus walking on water, calming the storm, raising the dead, feeding 5,000 people from five loaves and two fish would have caused onlookers to wonder whether they were seeing things, or had accidentally been drinking the stronger wine.

---

[2] The TV Tropes website calls this 'No More For Me': <https://tvtropes.org/pmwiki/pmwiki.php/Main/NoMoreForMe>.

Having heard them all their lives, many Christians are now very familiar with these stories. They are therefore no longer surprised by them. The inherent comedy of the subversion of the natural world has dissipated. Even at the time of Jesus' earthly ministry, onlookers and critics became quickly jaded and took the miracles for granted. Their blasé reaction is in itself funny.

For example, in John 11 we see reactions to the news that Jesus has raised Lazarus from the dead, which provoke a comic moment. The chief priests and the Pharisees, who bitterly oppose Jesus, are furious, saying, 'If we let him go on like this, everyone will believe in him, and then the Romans will come and take away both our place and our nation' (v. 48). Their reaction to the news that Jesus proves his power over life and death is not joy or amazement, or even begrudging respect, but irritation and panic.

How do you solve a problem like the Messiah?

As we read on in John 11, however, we see what the Sanhedrin council decide to do next, which is even funnier. They essentially say, 'Here is a man that's going around proving he has power over death itself. There's only one thing to do: kill him!' This does not sound like a good plan. They are indeed thwarted at the resurrection.

Having been exposed to the extraordinary miracles of Jesus from a young age, many Christians have essentially been inoculated against seeing the humour in the Gospel accounts. G. K. Chesterton claims that Jesus hid his mirth, but the comedy was hiding in plain sight. The very incarnation of Jesus creates humorous situations, provoking shocked reactions like Lois Lane's in the original Superman movie.

But is that where the comedy ends? Did Jesus use comedy in his teaching? If he did, we will need to moderate further our understanding of key biblical texts which tell Christians to concentrate on the pure and the lovely.

17

Was Jesus funny?

There is no verse in the Bible which says 'Jesus laughed.' But is that because it's bad manners to laugh at your own jokes? Jesus was not greatly concerned with manners, although those around him were. In the Gospel accounts, we see how religious people tend to be far more sensitive to decency and etiquette than Jesus was. In short, Jesus upset a lot of Pharisees.

Casting stones

Jesus is being more transgressive than it appears at first sight. We might assume that everyone knew Jesus was one of the 'good guys' and the Pharisees were the baddies. After all, the words 'Pharisaic' and 'Pharisaical' have entered our language. They mean strictly observing religious rules and ceremonies without reference to the heart or spirit, or, by extension, self-righteous or hypocritical.

When we think of Pharisees today, we might bring to mind the stoning scene in Monty Python's *Life of Brian*, in which a religious authority figure is caught out by his own rule and killed by a hail of rocks for saying the word 'Jehovah'. It's a satisfying outcome because this legal pedant, brilliantly played by John Cleese, was preparing to stone someone else for blasphemy, and we feel that he fully deserves his fate.

It would be a mistake to assume that the Pharisees were an unpopular group of nit-pickers whom nobody much liked. Jesus' scathing criticisms of the Pharisees were necessarily part of the zeitgeist. Pharisees were widely respected for their observance of a higher standard of the Jewish law. Many would have viewed them fondly, the way our society still views nuns who have set themselves apart for God's service.

Despite their numbers and popularity, the Pharisees were not the dominant part of the political class. That would be the Sadducees, who were the party of the elites. Don't worry. Jesus was fair. He upset the Sadducees too.[1]

First-century Jerusalem, with its Pharisees, Sadducees, chief priests and teachers of the law and Roman rulers and authorities, created a social minefield where even angels would fear to tread. Therefore, everyone, including Jesus, was being closely watched. Perhaps we can identify with this in our current age, where the twitchfork mob will go after any minor indiscretion that is deemed to be politically incorrect or could be construed as 'hate speech'.

Jesus stepped into this highly charged situation and regularly found himself in awkward situations. Sometimes he engineered them himself. He wilfully consorted with social outcasts, like tax collectors and prostitutes, causing dismay among the respectable classes. Jesus did not make excuses. Quite the reverse. He took those opportunities to say things that made the situation worse and caused even more offence.

---

[1] For an example of this, have a look at Matthew 22.23–33. The Sadducees try to catch Jesus out with a ludicrously hypothetical situation about marriage after the resurrection of the dead. It's particularly comic given that the Sadducees did not believe in the resurrection of the dead. This really struck me as being funny when it was read aloud during a time of worship at the General Synod of the Church of England in York in July 2018. In the chamber of a few hundred people, including bishops and archbishops, I laughed out loud. I was the only one.

Jesus was prepared to upset people with his use of comedy, parody and satire in his teaching ministry. Let us look at the various techniques he employed.[2]

Cartoon imagery

In Matthew 6, Jesus talks about giving to the needy and paints a cartoonish picture of this being done with a fanfare of trumpets. It feels like something from a Warner Brothers cartoon, and it's a comic image.

Jesus goes on to highlight those hypocrites' public displays of praying on street corners, and talks about their sombre and disfigured faces when they fast. It's not hard to imagine Jesus slipping into an impersonation and the listeners falling about laughing at what is essentially observational comedy.

Jesus uses comic exaggeration in Matthew 7.1–5 when he talks about those who see the faults of others but are blind to their own. He says, 'Why do you see the speck that is in your brother's eye, but do not notice the log that is in your own eye?' But Jesus doesn't stop there. All stand-up comedians know that once you establish a comic idea, you make the most of it. Jesus goes on, 'How can you say to your brother, "Let me take the speck out of your eye," when there is the log in your own eye?' It's funny to think of someone with a huge log in their eye stopping someone else to patiently explain to them that there's a piece of sawdust in their eye.

Later in Matthew, in chapter 23, Jesus uses a similar kind of joke to expose the hypocrisy of the Pharisees, saying that the way

---

[2] Jesus' use of comedy is not often mentioned in Christian literature but is highlighted in a slim but useful book, now out of print, called *The Humor of Christ* by Elton Trueblood. (Yes, he really is called Elton Trueblood. With a name like that, he should be writing Gothic fiction, but instead he chose to write a book demonstrating that Jesus employed comedy far more often than it first appears; Elton Trueblood, *The Humor of Christ* (New York: Harper and Row, 1964).)

to decide which laws to keep and which to ignore is hypocritical. He says they strain out a gnat and swallow a camel. It is another cartoonish image.

Luke reports Jesus teaching how fathers don't, when asked for an egg, give their children scorpions (Luke 11.11). It's an incongruous image that's as shocking as it is funny, but Jesus doesn't mind that. He shows this by going on to tell the crowd that even they, 'who are evil', wouldn't give their children scorpions. Jesus was not trying to make friends.

Creative insults

Modern-day Christians who only want to focus on the lovely and the pure run the risk of trying to be holier than Jesus. Jesus' use of insults showed that he was comfortable with name-calling. Twice in Matthew's Gospel, Jesus calls Pharisees 'vipers', a reference to evil satanic serpents (12.34; 23.33). He also calls them 'whitewashed tombs, which outwardly appear beautiful, but within are full of dead people's bones and all uncleanness' (23.27). The language of Matthew 23 is not meek, mild, lovely or pure. It is an all-out assault on hypocrisy, more reminiscent of comedians like Lenny Bruce and Bill Hicks.

Does this mean Christians are free to call anyone names, simply because Jesus used insults? No. Jesus did not flame every Pharisee and Sadducee in sight. Sometimes, he was gentle. One notable example is in Luke 7, where Jesus is dining at the house of a Pharisee called Simon. There is an embarrassing incident in which a 'sinful woman' finds her way to Jesus and anoints his feet with perfume. Simon responds with confusion and disgust. He says to himself, 'If this man were a prophet, he would have known who and what sort of woman this is who is touching him, for she is a sinner' (Luke 7.39).

Jesus, using comic understatement, says that he has something to tell Simon. He goes on to tell a short parable which reveals, with the greatest of respect, that Simon has got everything completely wrong. Jesus' criticism of his host would have been very difficult to take. The entire incident is painfully embarrassing.

Jesus often moderates his speech depending on the situation, person and message. Sometimes he is serious, sometimes tender, but always truthful. He can also be sassy, as with the Syrophoenician woman in Mark 7, a Gentile whom Jesus called a 'dog'. He must have known she could handle it and give as good as she got.[3] And she did. An exchange follows that these days would be called 'banter'.

That was uncalled for

What we're seeing in the Bible, from the mouth of Elijah, from the pen of Paul and from the lips of Jesus, are words and phrases that caused offence. These words are not being taken out of context. The speakers or writers of these words were not trying to avoid upsetting anyone. They were using strong language, difficult ideas or humiliating imagery in order to make a point.

What this should mean for Christians today is this: offence is a poor measure of the appropriateness of a joke. In other words, just because you are offended, it does *not* mean the joker should not have told the joke or used a particular word. In causing offence or embarrassment, the joker has not *necessarily* committed a sin. You are a flawed human being, so your judgement will not be as impeccable as that of Jesus, but the words may well be entirely justified, moral and apposite.

The flipside

The reverse of this is also true. Just because a joke did *not* cause offence, it does not make it okay or morally acceptable. The Syrophoenician woman in Mark 7 was called a 'dog'. I believe Jesus was using the word ironically, but it is quite likely that the

---

[3] There are many ways of reading this incident in Mark 7.28. There is no way that Jesus would have really thought that Gentiles were dogs, since his inclusion of Gentiles and outsiders in his kingdom is one of its key features.

Jewish audience were not offended by that remark and did not hear the irony. I would suggest they *should* have been offended! Their lack of offence was not a good sign.

In the same way, an anti-Semitic joke told at a neo-Nazi rally would probably have gone down well and caused little offence. This clearly does not make the joke acceptable. It just so happens there was no one in the room to take offence. The joke was probably told on that basis. But it demonstrates that the level of offence taken says little about the righteousness of the joke, merely the righteousness – or lack thereof – of the audience. Therefore, offensiveness should not be used to as the sole criterion of whether or not a joke should have been told.

Dear BBC

TV and radio broadcasters will tell you that in their experience Christians are easily offended and likely to complain about what they see or hear, but not all Christians complain. The number of complaints received on even the most provocative of programmes is usually measured in dozens rather than thousands. In the next chapter, we will see that a controversial Comic Relief sketch garnered 487 complaints to Ofcom, the TV regulator.

In Part 3, we will look at the case of *Jerry Springer: The Opera*, which was a show some Christians found highly offensive, with some justification. Even then, after a co-ordinated campaign to encourage Christians to complain about the BBC's broadcast of the show with careful instructions on how to do it, the complaints only ran into the tens of thousands. This is a small proportion of the total number of Christians in the UK, however you count them.

I did not complain to the BBC about the broadcast of *Jerry Springer: The Opera*, for reasons I will explain in more detail later. But one of the reasons is the material we have been considering in the Bible, with all its offensive language and imagery, often on the lips of Christ himself. Christians should know better than to cry 'foul' on the basis of being offended.

The problem with religious people

Another look at the Gospels reveals something else very troubling about religious people. Who were the ones who subjected Jesus to torture and death? Religious people. Highly offended religious people who successfully whipped up the crowds to agree with them.

Pharisees, Sadducees, teachers of the law and scribes had their differences but they could agree on one thing. That Jesus was a blasphemer.[4] Shocked and appalled at the blasphemous things Jesus had said, and the ridicule and scorn he heaped on them, they demanded satisfaction. They decided to kill the One with power over death itself. What's more, in another comic irony, they had the crowd call for the release of Barabbas, a well-known terrorist and murderer.

God became a man and lived a perfect life, healing the sick and raising the dead, and religious people killed him. It wasn't so-called 'sinners' who demanded his blood. It was the upright and the respectable. They are very easily offended. They do not shrug it off. They don't roll their eyes and wander away. They demand vengeance. It's not pretty.

Should Christians just stop complaining? When they are offended or embarrassed by a joke, should they just 'get over it'?

Not necessarily. Expressing one's dissatisfaction with a joke is often valid, especially when it seems to be unjust. Christians often feel that their faith is an easy target for comedians and the media. Why should that be?

---

[4] In fact, according to Luke 23.12, Jesus' trial and death sentence united Herod and Pilate, who until that point had been enemies.

18

Why Christianity is an easy target

In March 2013, Rowan Atkinson played the part of a cynical Archbishop of Canterbury who said that prayer doesn't work. It was a Comic Relief sketch for a pre-watershed BBC audience. Many Christians did not find this joke funny and were offended, prompting 487 of them to complain to the TV regulator, Ofcom. Ofcom responded to the complaints a few months later, saying the BBC had not breached broadcasting codes.

To be fair, that same month the BBC aired a documentary presenting a more conservative view of religion and comedy. It was authored by former Tory MP Ann Widdecombe, who argued that modern comedy is too blasphemous. In the *Daily Telegraph*, she wrote, 'Gentle mockery or sharp satire aimed at Christians and their leaders have been replaced by abuse of Christianity itself.'[1]

Many British Christians would sympathize with Widdecombe's thesis. They are accustomed to having their faith made the butt of jokes, the Comic Relief sketch being a case in point. They are still angry and confused about this. Given that only around 10 per cent of the population regularly attend church, how can the continual lampooning of this small minority be morally justified? Isn't it just bullying?

---

[1] 'Christians Are the Butt of Bad Jokes', *Daily Telegraph*, 27 March 2013: <www.telegraph.co.uk/lifestyle/9957059/Ann-Widdecombe-Christians-are-the-butt-of-bad-jokes.html>.

State of the nation

One might argue that the UK is still a Christian country, but the faith is hardly the preserve of rich elites. They abandoned the Christian faith decades, even centuries, ago. Even G. K. Chesterton was fighting rear-guard ideological battles against influential atheists like George Bernard Shaw at the turn of the previous century. Given the demographic changes in the UK since the Second World War, a professing Christian now is just as likely to be a Pentecostal black single mother or a Catholic Polish bricklayer[2] as an Evangelical white middle-class professional and father of two. How is attacking the faith of people like this seen to be acceptable or even righteous?

There are a few factors at play here. The first is the weight of history and heritage that comes with the Christian faith. Those who attend church faithfully on Sunday may be a small minority now, but that was not the case in the West for centuries. The Church was only an underground and persecuted movement for a few hundred years. When the Roman emperor Constantine the Great became a Christian in AD 312, everything changed. Christianity became not only tolerated, but the official religion of the establishment.

Even though the Roman empire was beginning to crumble, the Christian faith was firmly established, making inroads in Britain even before Augustine arrived with his Benedictine monks in 597. The only issue for the next 1,000 years or so was which kind of Christianity would be the mainstream.

The first choice was between Roman or Celtic Christianity. The Romans won that one at the Synod of Whitby in AD 664. Nearly 1,000 years later, in 1534, the Romans lost when England left the Church of Rome in favour of an English form of Protestantism.

---

[2] According to a report by the IPPR, 'Catholicism has been boosted by the arrival of almost 600,000 immigrants from Poland, Lithuania and Slovakia': <www.telegraph.co.uk/news/religion/6799755/Study-reveals-impact-of-immigration-on-UK-faiths.html>.

Soon afterwards, the Catholic and Protestant West exported their respective faiths to the 'New Worlds' via missionaries, conquistadors and colonial rule. The dominance of Christianity continued unabated. Established Christian faith may have declined during the Enlightenment, but it remains embedded in the structures of power, for centuries after and up to today.

In the UK, at least, the monarch is still the Supreme Governor of the Church of England, a role that is more than ceremonial, especially as Queen Elizabeth II is more vocal about her own Christian faith. Bishops still sit in the House of Lords, purely by dint of being Anglican bishops. Schools are still required by the state to give some kind of religious instruction or act of worship. The national broadcaster, the BBC, is still required to make religious programmes, and the *Today* programme still has a 'Thought for the Day' every morning at peak time (even though the deep resentment of this slot by the presenters is obvious).

The power of prayer

Therefore, a joke on national TV in which the Archbishop of Canterbury appears to be feckless and faithless can be considered, with some justification, as part of attacking the establishment. The comedians are 'sticking it to the man'.

The joke rang rather hollow to Christians, who knew that 'the man' on this occasion was Justin Welby, the Archbishop of Canterbury at the time. He is clearly a man who believes in the power of prayer[3] and regularly articulates a meaningful, personal Christian faith.

The joke seemed to be a generic one about the establishment and the office rather than Archbishop Justin's own theological views. The Archbishop of Canterbury is a public figure. Being the butt of jokes is part of the job. But what about the people in the pews, who often feel powerless?

---

[3] One need only look at his public 'Thy Kingdom Come' prayer campaign.

Familiarity breeds contempt

Non-Christian comedians might argue that in the most recent UK census, in 2011, 'Christianity remained the largest religion with 59.3 per cent of the population identifying themselves as Christian. Muslims made up the second largest religious group with 4.8 per cent of the population.'[4] That's still a majority of people identifying as Christian when 'No religion' was also an option.

Jonathan Miller, the satirist and theatre director, famously said that 'I'm not really a Jew, just Jew-ish.' In the same way, it might be fair to say that the UK may no longer be Christian, but Christian-ish. Churchgoing Christians may not feel as if they have any kind of political or cultural influence, but their faith is still embedded in the power structures and people of the nation. Therefore, comedians could feel justified in thinking that the Church, the Christian faith or Christians are fair game. They can be kicked in the crotch with a clear conscience.

The Christian faith is still a punchbag for another crucial reason that means Christianity is comparative easy to lampoon, whereas other faiths are not. We will look at why in the next chapter.

---

[4] <www.ons.gov.uk/peoplepopulationandcommunity/culturalidentity/religion/articles/religioninenglandandwales2011/2012-12-11>.

19

Why don't comedians make jokes about Islam?

Hello. If you're a Christian, this might well be the first chapter of the book you turned to. You might be sitting on the loo and idly flicking through someone else's copy of this book, and this is the question that grabbed your attention. That would not be a surprise, as Christians ask this question an awful lot.

If this is where you are starting in the book, can I suggest reading the previous chapters first? You might need to take up residency in the downstairs loo if that is where you are reading it, although it might be less embarrassing to buy a copy for yourself and read it elsewhere. But previous chapters will put in place a few things that we're going to continue here.

We noted Ann Widdecombe's *Daily Telegraph* article from 2013 about her problem with the mockery of her Christian faith. Sure enough, as Christians normally do when feeling under siege, she compared Christianity and Islam as targets, writing:

> After all, comedy producers respect Islam sufficiently to avoid laughing at the Prophet so why are even the most sacred aspects of this country's major faith seemingly the stuff of so much comedy? Is it because the Church here is seen as part of the Establishment?[1]

---

[1] 'Christians Are the Butt of Bad Jokes', *Daily Telegraph*, 27 March 2013: <www.telegraph.co.uk/lifestyle/9957059/Ann-Widdecombe-Christians-are-the-butt-of-bad-jokes.html>.

The answer to this last questions would be 'yes', as we saw in the last chapter. She goes on: 'Or is it due to the rise of militant atheism? Or is it simply that comics would be afraid to do to Islam that which they regularly do in their routines to Christianity?'

Answering her valid concern about the apparent injustice of the situation, we need to begin by understanding that it is easier to make jokes about Christianity than Islam for one simple reason: jokes rely on shared information. (We considered this in Part 1 of this book. You'll need to go back and read that too. Sorry.) Despite its decline in political power and widespread adherents, Christianity still provides numerous shared cultural reference points around which jokes, routines and sketches can be based.

Comedy landscapes

At Christmas, for example, jokes can be made about a nativity scene in which most people understand that there are wise men, shepherds, angels, a star and a baby in a manger. Although the details and significance of the Easter story are, sadly, much more obscure, it is still widely understood that Jesus was a teacher and miracle worker, who rose from the dead, healed the sick, fed 5,000 people and turned water into wine.

Watch *Glorious*, a stand-up show by Eddie Izzard from 1997, and you will see him draw heavily on well-known Bible tales. There are lengthy routines about the creation of the world, Noah building his ark and the nativity story.

Likewise, church rites and practice provide plenty of settings in which chaos can be created and incongruity presented. An obvious example would be a sketch in the BBC comedy *Goodness Gracious Me* (1998–2001) in which an Indian couple who don't understand how Holy Communion works attempt to put mango chutney on the wafer.[2]

---

[2] In her BBC documentary, Ann Widdecombe, who converted to Roman Catholicism in 1993, took particular exception to this sketch since to her during

Even 20 years on from that sketch, despite a general decline in church attendance, one might still see a sketch in which a vicar is baptizing a baby in a church font. There were 120,000 Church of England baptisms in 2016, each attended by one or two parents and a few godparents. That's at least half a million people witnessing a baptism in 2016 alone. Add to this 45,000 marriages in Church of England churches, 139,000 Church of England-led funerals, the Christmas tradition of going to church, and we still have several million people walking into churches and taking part in some kind of Christian service.

This means that you can still do jokes and sketches about christenings, church weddings and funerals and be confident you will carry the audience with you. These are particularly good scenarios for sketches because they are significant life moments that need to be done with dignity and respect. People are wearing special clothes and have assigned roles. From a comedic point of view, this is very fertile soil. No wonder one of the most successful and acclaimed comedies in British movie history is *Four Weddings and a Funeral.*

Let us now ask this question: what are the similar or equivalent sacred rituals for Muslims that could form the basis for sketches? What does a Muslim wedding ceremony look like? Do Muslims have a version of baptism? What about funerals? How are they conducted? What is widely known about Islam's prophet Muhammad? What happens in a mosque? What are the precise rules for Ramadan? It is easy to see why this does not seem to be such promising ground for comedy.

Spot the difference

Comedy depends on simplicity, as well as familiarity. Extraneous information needs to be removed in order for the components

the Mass the wafer becomes the very body of Christ. At the time, regulators frowned on the *Goodness Gracious Me* Communion sketch and the BBC has been forbidden from repeating it. Perhaps such a sketch would be permitted now.

of the joke to be clear. A brief scan of international newspapers will quickly reveal there are varieties of Islam that do not agree with one another. This makes life more complicated. So when one makes a joke about Islam, what kind of Islam is one joking about? Shia? Sunni? Wahabi?

Comedy about such divisions is possible. There is a delightful song by Richard Stilgoe and Peter Skellern called 'The Curate and the Priest' in which an Anglican curate and a Catholic priest competitively sing at each other before acknowledging at the end that no one goes to either of their churches. The implication is that the divisions they are so proud of are a turn-off to the general public.

The differences between denominations in the UK were kept very clear given the deep divisions in Northern Ireland over several decades. Comedians made full use of the political characters to put faces to the different denominations. For many years, staunch Protestantism could be represented by Ian Paisley, as it was on ITV's satirical smash, *Spitting Image*. In fact, everyone could have a go at an Ian Paisley impersonation.[3] *Spitting Image* also had a memorable Catholic representative figure in the 'rock star'-style pope John Paul II. Such stereotypes are crude but at least provide a backdrop for jokes about Christianity, Catholicism, Protestantism and sectarianism in general.

One might also be able to do jokes on even more specific forms of Protestantism, such as members of the Salvation Army, who help the homeless, wear uniforms and still form brass bands. Puritans easily can be depicted as dour ascetics, such as Lord and Lady Whiteadder in *Blackadder II*. We might also be able to summon up images to parody with the words 'Pentecostal preacher'. Consider the scene featuring James Brown from the 1980 classic *The Blues Brothers*. Whether these stereotypes are justified is a separate issue. The point is that there is enough cultural

---

[3] This usually involved emphatically saying, 'No!'

weight to them to make jokes about various kinds of Christianity possible.

This is not the case with Islam. With the relatively recent influx of Muslims into the UK, comedy about the faith of the average Muslim is extremely hard given the lack of knowledge and reference points. You simply would not be able to do jokes about Islam with respect to divisions about the Shia, Sunni and Wahabi traditions, to name only three, without sending out lengthy and contentious fact sheets in advance. This is not a good recipe for comedy.

Je suis Charlie

It's very difficult, then, to make jokes about something that is not widely understood. Most comedians and comedy writers, therefore, don't bother. This isn't so much bias or fear, as Widdecombe alleges, but basic comedy mechanics.

It is easy to say that comedians are afraid to mock Islam, but if you've ever met a comedian you'll know that they are often very happy with confrontation or controversy. They do not temperamentally veer away from hot topics. Quite the reverse.[4]

Moreover, some comedians *do* make jokes about Islam. *Charlie Hebdo*, the French satirical magazine, a secular and sceptical publication, prides itself on criticizing *all* religions, Islam included. After news of the introduction of Sharia law in Libya and the victory of the Islamist party in Tunisia, the 3 November 2011 edition was renamed 'Charia Hebdo', with Muhammad listed as the 'editor-in-chief'. Shortly afterwards, the offices in Paris were firebombed. The cartoonists were not deterred. More jokes at the expense of Islam and its prophet followed, culminating in the armed attack of 7 January 2015 in which 12 members of staff were shot dead by two Islamist gunmen.

---

[4] Those wishing to know more about the minds of comedians should listen to Stuart Goldsmith's excellent podcast, 'Comedian's Comedian', at <www.comedianscomedian.com>.

Not just the few

Given the chilling effect of reprisals, one might think that *Charlie Hebdo* stands alone in its comedy around Islam, but that isn't true. On the British comedy circuit there are a number of Muslim comedians who talk about Islam, the practice and the community of its believers. Bilal Zafar has been performing since 2013 and has been nominated for numerous awards. One could also mention Tez Ilyas, Sadia Azmat, Jay Islaam and Aatif Nawaz.[5]

This is the preserve not just of the comedy club but also of national broadcasters. BBC1 has aired five series of *Citizen Khan* (2012–17),[6] a sitcom about a Muslim family, headed by the vain social climber, Mr Khan, who likes to position himself as a 'community leader'. Naturally it has attracted criticism for being unrepresentative of Muslim culture but, given it is only one family, how could it reflect the diverse lives of British Muslims?

The notion, then, that jokes cannot be, and are not, made about Islam is not quite true. They may not be common, but why should they be? According to the 2011 census only 4.4 per cent of the UK population identified as Muslim. Although Islam claims hundreds of millions of adherents globally, it is not a mainstream religion in the UK. Moreover, that 4.4 per cent is four times what it was as recently as 1981, when Muslims made up only 1.1 per cent of the population. Some may argue that Muslims 'punch above their weight' in terms of culture, while it probably doesn't feel that way to British Muslims, who are just as tired of comedy stereotypes of themselves as Christians are.

As the demographics of a nation changes, the jokes will change with them. Because of their cultural heritage and dominance, Christians have been easy and often justifiable targets for jokes. These jokes may dwindle if Christianity continues to decline in the West, or become more prevalent if there is revival.

---

[5] <http://mvslim.com/5-muslim-comedians-taking-britains-comedy-scene/>.
[6] I co-wrote two episodes with Adil Ray for Series 5.

Either way, the vast and lasting legacy of Christianity in the UK, at least, ensures that jokes will continue to be made about Jesus, God, the Church and the Bible for many years to come. We may wish to point out they are offensive, or claim they are unfair, as Ann Widdecombe has done. This may well be justified but can look sour or resentful and contribute to the assumption that the Church has a sense of humour problem. Do we really want to be seen as Jorges and Mary Whitehouses? What can the Church practically do to change this image? The answer, ironically, does not begin with jokes.

20

Why you shouldn't start a sermon with a joke

Dave Allen was a brilliant comedian. He was not quite a stand-up comedian because he usually sat down. The majority of his TV shows were comic monologues, but there would also be a few sketches. These regularly featured church situations, normally Catholic ones. They would often depict priests, sometimes the Pope, behaving badly or child-ishly. For example, one features the Pope with his cardinals on the steps of St Peter's, undressing to the music 'The Stripper'. By now, we can see that these kinds of sketches are funny because churches are considered to be serious places so there is great comic incongruity.

Churches are places where people feel the need to be on their best behaviour. In many cases, churches are ancient buildings with stained-glass depictions of saints. But it is not just heritage and art that contributes to the sense of propriety. Non-conformist churches can also have their own kind of austerity. Sometimes the Ten Commandments are written on the wall facing the congrega-tion, and you sit there with these words denoting your own fail-ings and flaws bearing down on you. One church I attended had the following in large letters: 'What Think Ye of Christ?' Churches are not buildings in which one expects to laugh.

There is more to the culture of the Church as a whole than what happens in a Sunday service, but this hour or so spent in the presence of one another before God is very significant. If we're looking for the Church to rehabilitate comedy and change her image, shouldn't we want sermons, at least, to be funnier? What better way to start a sermon than with a joke?

A vicar walks into a pulpit . . .

Lots of preachers like to start their sermons this way or with a light-hearted anecdote. They do this to break the ice, warm up the congregation and show outsiders that they have a sense of humour. Initially, this sounds like a good idea. But I would advise against it. There are many reasons why.

First, we have already seen in Part 1 the myriad of ways in which jokes can go wrong. Telling a joke to a congregation, some of whom might be visitors or strangers, is a high-risk strategy. The joke may fall flat, which takes the wind out of the preacher's sails. Or it may offend unnecessarily, which renders the rest of the sermon suspect. Far from establishing one's credentials, the joke could destroy trust, which is vital if one wishes to preach effectively.

There are other reasons for my concerns on starting with a joke,[1] but here is the one most relevant to the matter in hand: it undermines the idea that comedy can be found in Scripture itself. If the preacher repeatedly uses his or her own comic gifts and gets the congregation to laugh, what does that say about the comic potency of the Scriptures?

Over time, the impression is given that any laughter in church will only ever come from the preacher and never from the Bible itself. This will perpetuate the stereotype that the Bible is always sombre and stern, when that is not the case. The result will be that comedy will continue to be seen as a deviation from Scripture, and something transgressive, like the funny song in a musical, rather than the natural outworking of the Scriptures.

---

[1] For a longer treatment of this subject, see here: <www.jamescary.co.uk/comedy/it-got-a-laugh/>.

If the Church is going to rehabilitate comedy, it has to come from the foundational document, the Bible, and the founder, Jesus Christ. But how is this to be done?

Musical matters

Let us take a brief step sideways into music, something that many churches, large and small, take very seriously. Cathedrals have choristers' schools set up to provide willing voices for their choirs, under the baton of choirmasters and directors of music. Small churches might expect to pay something for the services of a trained organist. Larger, more lively churches have enormous sound desks and miles of cables plugged into multiple instruments. They may even employ a 'worship leader'. Other churches will make do with the expertise around them.

A lot of effort and care is taken to ensure that the music in churches is as good as it can be. There is an expectation this will cost money and require trained or experienced practitioners, if not full-time staff. No one expects someone with no experience of playing the organ, piano or guitar to step forward and lead the congregation in their singing.

This is not the case with the public reading of Scripture. Reading the lesson on a Sunday morning is normally put on a rota and thought of as a job to be done, like opening up the building before the service or making the coffee afterwards. It is certainly not on a par with musical worship. Sometimes, it is thought to be a good way of involving people in the service who might otherwise feel underused.

As long as the reading of Scripture remains an after-thought in most church services, the wider Church will never rediscover the literary richness of the Bible, especially the comic themes and moments. These become obvious when you hear Scripture read extremely well, having been rehearsed and memorized and then presented with confidence. On those occasions, something remarkable happens. People laugh.

Permission to laugh

I first became aware of the power of pure Scripture when I saw a performance by former Broadway actor Bruce Kuhn. He had learned one of the Gospels by heart. He did not change a letter of the text, but studied it, thought about it, rehearsed it and brought his skills to bear on the task of performing it. He told the Gospel story as if he had just heard it and was passing it on. As he did so, the audience could feel the story, notice the comic incongruities, hear the comic repetitions and understand the absurdities of God becoming human, and the reactions of the disciples, the crowds and the priests to his power and authority.

The skills of actors are not just useful here but essential. The culture that wrote the Scriptures themselves, both the Old and New Testaments, would have expected the words to be read aloud to a crowd rather than silently studied alone. Scripture is a script. It comes alive when read aloud. Our ears are engaged rather than our eyes, leaving our minds to create pictures. Rather than processing words, we can see people and places, experiencing the stories described as if we were there.

I've watched Bruce perform many times, to the point where I now watch the audience watch Bruce. Initially, they feel as though they can't laugh, or that laughing is an inappropriate reaction, especially if the performance takes place in a church. But after a while, they just can't help it. They don't laugh at everything, obviously. The Gospels are not really comedies – although they do have a comic structure in that they have a happy ending. And we have already seen how they have comic elements and moments.

Lend me your ears

Shakespeare's plays are 400 years old and in a recognizable form of English with comprehensible situations. The latest parts of the Bible describe events which took place 2,000 years ago under the Roman occupation of Palestine. But there is also material from the Israelites' captivity in Babylon and their slavery in Egypt, hundreds and thousands of years earlier. The Bible is a very foreign country.

Anyone who has lived in a foreign country will know that it is hard enough to understand the language and the customs. The sense of humour is normally the hardest thing of all to comprehend and navigate – let alone use safely and convincingly. The potential for offence and misunderstanding is enormous.

When one watches Shakespeare's plays performed well, the differences in language and customs rapidly melt away. Physical action, body language and vocal tone go a long way to mitigating the unfamiliar turns of phrase.

All of the above require effort, rehearsal and training. But none of these things come about in isolation. There is now a tradition of open-air Shakespeare plays that tour the country over the summer months with their productions of *A Midsummer Night's Dream* or *As You Like It*. There is also a permanent home for Shakespeare's plays, the Globe, on the South Bank in London, that aims to recapture the feeling of being at an original Shakespearean play. Performing at the Globe is now a professional aspiration for many young actors and actresses, just as many great actors long to be given the honour of performing Hamlet.

The result is a culture of Shakespearean theatre that seeks excellence. When one goes to see any performance of a Shakespeare play, one rightly has high expectations of enjoyment. If it's a comedy one expects to laugh, despite Shakespeare's world being unfamiliar to us.

Culture shifts

In order to rediscover and re-present the richness of the biblical texts, which would help Christians see the comedy inherent in the Scriptures, there needs to be a change in the culture within the Church. This could involve a rediscovery of the long-lost theatrical traditions of mystery plays that died out in the Reformation. Perhaps, one day, Christian actors might be inspired to perform

Scripture even more than Shakespeare. Others could use their gifts to train Scripture-readers to do this better, just as there are many who seek to equip musicians use their gifts more effectively in the service of the Church.

The result would be a renaissance in a Christian kind of comedy rooted in the Bible, rather than a comic tradition that runs alongside it and occasionally against it. The latter is where starting a sermon with a joke leads. The preacher becomes comedian. This is not progress.

The Church needs an antidote for the barbed and pointed jokes made at her expense, some of which are undoubtedly justified. For a shift in culture to be sustainable, this revival must spring from the foundational document, the Bible, rather than individually gifted 'preaching comedians'.

In the final chapter of this section, then, we will take a look at a few more examples of comedy tucked away in the Bible which could and should become clearer when read out loud. We will also think about how to 'find the funny' in those passages. There are obvious limitations to explaining the written word using other written words so please also consult my website, <www.jamescary. co.uk>, for links to videos which will illustrate what I mean more clearly. But for now, let us press on with the written version.

21

Notes for readers

S*herlock*, the TV series created by Stephen Moffat and Mark Gatiss, is mysterious and exhilarating. It is also funny. Moffat used to write sitcoms (*Coupling, Joking Apart*) and Gatiss was part of the award-winning *League of Gentlemen* sketch group. The scripts are undoubtedly excellent and funny. But where does the audience find itself laughing?

The laughs might not come quite where you're expecting. Sherlock Holmes, as played by Benedict Cumberbatch, is a comedy character. He is astonishingly observant, deductive and intuitive, while understanding so little about people and human interaction. Essentially, he's super-smart but very rude. The bit where you laugh, though, is when Watson reacts. As Watson, Martin Freeman is truly brilliant at reacting. As a hobbit being descended upon by dwarfs or an office worker coping with an annoying boss called David Brent, Freeman has shown that he is probably the best 'reactor' in the business.

Good comedy TV directors know that you don't just point the camera at the funny person. You make sure you get a shot of the onlooker or the other guy. When you think about it, this is just an extension of our theory that comedy stems from incongruity, placing the funny person next to the straight man. When we show that abnormal, we sometimes need to remind the audience of the normal to get the laugh.

Notes for readers

Donkey business

Bear this 'reacting' in mind when one reads aloud some of the most overtly comic passages in Scripture. One such passage would be the story of Balaam's donkey, to be found in the book of Numbers, chapter 22. Balaam, a prophet of God, has been asked by some Moabites to curse the Egyptians who are attacking them. They want him to act as a spiritual hitman. Balaam eventually agrees, despite God expressly telling him not to do so. Nevertheless, he sets out the next day and saddles his donkey and they ride off. But on a narrow path in a vineyard, the donkey sees an angel blocking their path. Trying to avoid the angel, the donkey bashes Balaam's foot against a wall. Balaam can't see the angel, or will not, assumes the donkey is being disobedient, and beats her. This is all repeated when the donkey sees the angel again and, unable to turn, sits down.

We already have a funny image. The slow-witted donkey can see the angel and is attempting to take evasive action. And Balaam, the stubborn prophet of God, cannot. The donkey is the wise one here since she fears the Lord.

It gets worse for Balaam because 'Then the LORD opened the mouth of the donkey, and she said to Balaam, "What have I done to you, that you have struck me these three times?"' (Numbers 22.28).

This is the moment to 'react'. Take a lesson from Martin Freeman. If you're reading this passage aloud, pause here. Let what is happening sink into the listeners. Think about Balaam's first reaction here. A donkey is talking to him. This is not normal. We sometimes assume that our ancestors were rather backward, but they knew donkeys didn't talk. So pause. Have Balaam think about what's happening.

Balaam's response, however, is not what you might expect. Confronted with a talking donkey today, you would probably exclaim, 'My donkey is talking!' or you might seek psychiatric help. Not Balaam. He is so stubborn – and donkey-like – that he engages in a conversation with his donkey. He says, 'Because you have made a fool of me. I wish I had a sword in my hand, for then I would kill you.' Let us leave Balaam there, screaming at his donkey and move on.

The story we've just read is self-evidently comic – a donkey is talking – but a little obscure, tucked away in the neglected book of Numbers. The title alone is not terribly inviting. But we don't need to go to the overlooked parts of the Bible. We can find humour in better-known passages of Scripture that are often read or quoted. Let's look at a couple.

Moses and the burning bush

A key part in the history of Israel, the burning bush scene in Exodus 3—4 would be easy to paint as august and sombre. God is speaking to Moses from a bush that is on fire but not being consumed by it. The great Moses is being given this special mission to release God's people from slavery in Egypt. Someone called to read this passage aloud in church might assume it's essential to look and sound deadly serious. But there are plenty of clues to show that this scene is dysfunctionally comic.

Let us first bear in mind the context. Moses is hot-headed, having a killed a man in Exodus 2.12. He is also a coward, having fled Egypt when it turned out some people knew what he had done. He also knows the Pharaoh, does not fancy his chances and does not want to go back to Egypt. He is full of excuses.

He says he can't go in God's name because he doesn't know God's name. So God reveals his name, Yahweh. Does Moses respond with repentance and faith? No, he brings out more sick notes. The Egyptians won't listen to him, he says. So God shows his power by changing Moses' staff into a snake.

Does Moses stand there marvelling at God's power? No. He runs from the snake! It's a human response, but the wrong one. Given the mission he has in mind for Moses, God's hardly going to poison him, although it would be tempting given the further excuses. Moses says he's not good at speaking in public. God reminds Moses that he is the One who made Moses' mouth. Surely, that's game, set and match to Yahweh? Doesn't Moses have to give in? No. After all of the above, read Exodus 4.13. Moses says, 'Oh, my Lord, please send someone else.'

That's funny. God is trying to envision and empower his servant to do great things and perform amazing signs. And the servant is not having any of it. The chapters are reminiscent of the calling of Gideon in Judges 6. The Lord tells Gideon he is going to save Israel from the Midianites. Gideon replies, 'Behold, my clan is the weakest in Manasseh, and I am the least in my father's house' (v. 15). It's surprising he doesn't also claim to have an old sporting injury as well as jury duty that he just can't get out of.

Taking the time

If one is going to read Scripture aloud in church, it takes time and effort to unearth these moments. They may not be visible on a first or even second reading. Some lines are *only* funny when you think about them a little. Take Adam's line to God in the Garden of Eden in Genesis 3.12. It's another serious scene. It's the aftermath of the fall of humankind. God calls Adam and asks if he has eaten from the tree he was specifically told not to eat from. Does Adam man up and take responsibility? No. He blames everyone but himself, which is impressive given he only knows two people, Eve and God. So he says, 'The woman whom *you* gave to be with me, *she* gave me fruit of the tree, and I ate.' Wow. That's some impressive wriggling, worthy of a snake.

Using the mind's eye

Picture yourself at the wedding in Cana in John 2 when Jesus turns water into wine. Remember that this is the first miracle in John's Gospel. Jesus says his time has 'not yet come'. His mother ignores this and orders the servants to do whatever Jesus says. He tells them to fill six stone water jars and take some to the master of the feast.

Let's think about the poor servant shoved forward for that final task. He has to take a beaker of possibly diseased water to his boss's boss. You can imagine him cringing as he does this, as Jesus looks on, fully confident that all will be well. And it is. Imagine the relief of everyone when the water has become wine. Use the words of Scripture to tell that story.

Suppose you saw a film one night that you really enjoyed. You'd tell people about it the next day, wouldn't you? You would be overflowing with excitement, but also keen to ensure that you told the story correctly and that the listener was as excited by the story as you were. Why not employ a similar technique with reading Scripture? Like the timid servant with his beaker of water, you might be surprised at the results. One of those results will be the sound of genuine joyful laughter. The Church could really do with some of that if the image of Mary Whitehouse is going to be shaken off.

But is there no role for complaining and objecting to offensive jokes? There is indeed. In Scripture we not only see alarmingly ambiguous comic moments, but hear prophetic voices who speak up when no one listens or cares. If there is a time to laugh and a time to be silent, when is it time to speak? And how should it be done? That is what we will be covering in the final section of this book.

Building on the basic principles of Parts 1 and 2, we will see examples of how we can navigate comedy in the real world, where the stakes can be raised very quickly by the long arm of the law or angry men with guns. We're going to look at P. G. Wodehouse, laughing at funerals, Donald Trump, meta-jokes, *Family Guy*, Count Dankula, Mel Brooks and *Seinfeld,* and take a deep dive into *Jerry Springer: The Opera*, with a brief diversion into *Game of Thrones* before considering *The Book of Mormon*. We will finish by seeing how and why Easter is funny.

Part 3

ADVANCED JOKING

22

Betrayed by laughter

'But, Aunt Dahlia, listen to reason. I assure you, you've got
hold of the wrong man. I'm hopeless at a game like that. Ask
Jeeves about the time I got lugged in to address a girls' school.
I made the most colossal ass of myself.'

'And I confidently anticipate that you will make an equally
colossal ass of yourself on the thirty-first of this month. That's
why I want you. The way I look at it is that, as the thing is
bound to be a frost, anyway, one may as well get a hearty
laugh out of it.'[1]

Few understood comedy better than P. G. Wodehouse,
author of numerous novels and short stories which perfectly combine wit, character and farce. Wodehouse also
understood that comedy is unreliable. Jokes have a tendency to
go wrong.

In *Right Ho, Jeeves*,[2] Bertie Wooster is attempting to rekin-
dle love between Tuppy Glossop and Angela Travers, who have
recently had a tiff. He tells his butler, Jeeves, that his plan is to
'roast' Tuppy to Angela, 'giving it as my opinion that in all essen-
tials he is more like a wart hog than an ex-member of a fine old

---

[1] P. G. Wodehouse, *Right Ho, Jeeves* (London: Herbert Jenkins, 1934).

[2] Readers may be more familiar with the TV adaptation, which was Series 1,
Episode 5, 'Will Anatole Return to Brinkley Court?' First transmitted 20 May
1990.

English public school'. He says that this will awaken the 'maternal tigress' in Angela and she will leap to Tuppy's defence.

Wooster goes on to explain that he witnessed this phenomenon first hand in Antibes when he was invited by a girl to be rude about a young man who happened to be swimming. After being 'extraordinarily witty and satirical about this bird's underpinning', Wooster received all kinds of abuse from the girl, who realized her beloved swimmer was not so bad after all. Wooster goes on,

> This girl went on to dissect my manners, morals, intellect, general physique, and method of eating asparagus with such acerbity that by the time she had finished the best you could say of Bertram was that, so far as was known, he had never actually committed murder or set fire to an orphan asylum.

The couple were happily reconciled.

The point here, aside from revelling for a moment in the beautiful use of language by Wodehouse, is not that the path of love rarely runs smooth. We are more concerned with the path of comedy, which can be considerably bumpier. Wodehouse is highlighting that comedy and satire can reveal inner feelings about something or someone. These might be feelings that were hitherto unknown or unappreciated, certainly the case with the girl in Antibes. The moment her spurned lover was satirized, at her own invitation, she realized her love for him was deeper than she knew.

Lunch goes wrong

This can easily happen in a more mundane situation. Imagine three colleagues, Daphne, Elsie and Fred, on a lunchbreak in the staff kitchen, joking about their overbearing boss, Germaine, or a hopeless new intern. Elsie makes a joke that oversteps a line that no one had realized was there.

Suddenly, the joke is considered to be unjust, lunch is swiftly ended and Elsie has been blindsided by a sudden outbreak of mercy, kindness and disapproval. The Human Resources department gets wind of it and might feel the need to be seen to do something. Before Elsie knows what's happened, she's been sent on a course designed to help her be more considerate of her work colleagues.

On another day, the joke might have been received differently. Our feelings are inconsistent, as we saw in Part 1. We are moving cars. In the case of Tuppy and Angela, in *Right Ho, Jeeves*, Bertie's plan backfires badly. Bertie makes fun of Tuppy in his absence, but rather than take offence and leap to defend her former fiancé, Angela wholeheartedly agrees with Bertie's assertions, describing Tuppy as 'one of the six silliest asses in England'. We are not given the names of the other five.

Comedy has the power to awaken feelings of outrage or laughter. Either way, the response is immediate and vocal. Herein lies another reason that comedy is treated with grave suspicion by those in authority who are trying to project a serious image. A joke that is wrong or rude or disrespectful might elicit a laugh, rather than a frown or a scowl. A laugh is audible. It cannot be taken back. If you have worked for many years on an image of austerity, the last thing you want is to be seen laughing at the wrong thing. The spell will be broken for ever.

Comedy is based on truth. A guffaw may reveal that you hold something to be true that you have said with a straight face is not true. Or perhaps your sober face is required by your surroundings, at which point laughter is your enemy.

Triggering sniggers

Some of us will have experienced this when we get the giggles at a funeral. It's very unlikely to happen at a funeral of someone you truly loved because you really are devastated. But if you're there to support someone else, or you feel obliged to attend, something may happen that triggers a snigger. A relative (let's call her Auntie Barbara) has ludicrous hair. Or Uncle Bob is obviously wearing a toupee but is also looking very serious. The image is incongruous and you snigger. You immediately attempt to stifle this because to laugh at a funeral is incredibly insensitive. Spouses or siblings are clearly grieving. It looks bad.

But it gets worse. You get into a feedback loop of giggles. Why? You realize that this is the worst possible place to get the giggles. This is, in itself, funny. You can't stop wanting to giggle. You try to cover your mouth with a handkerchief and that just makes it worse. You giggle at your pathetic attempts to cover up your giggles. Perhaps you make eye contact with a friend who spots your giggling. She sees your predicament and starts giggling herself. Eventually, you make your excuses and leave, bursting out laughing at the far end of the graveyard or car park, hoping no one else has seen you.

What is happening in that funeral situation? After the initial giggle, you are laughing at the inappropriateness of the joke. You spot the absurdity, realize that laughing is in poor taste given the situation, and then you laugh at that new situation that has been created. Sometimes, you might not even remember what started you giggling in the first place. This phenomenon leads us into a kind of comedy that can be very problematic for those not in on the joke, or this style of humour.

Comedy New York style

In his book, *Win Bigly*,[3] Scott Adams writes about Donald Trump's 'New York' sense of humour and sees how easily it is misconstrued. For example, a joke Trump made about Senator John McCain was jaw-dropping for many people.

In McCain's own run for president in 2008, a great deal was made of his military service and capture during the Vietnam war

---

[3] Scott Adams, *Win Bigly: Persuasion in a World Where Facts Don't Matter* (London: Penguin, 2017).

in 1967. He spent five years in a prison camp. In short, McCain was a war hero, as his recent obituaries made very clear.

McCain criticized Trump during his election campaign in 2016. Trump responded while attending a Family Leadership Summit in Iowa,[4] saying of McCain, 'He's a war hero because he was captured. I like people who weren't captured.' Wow.

Scott Adams, being brought up not far from New York, wrote that he recognized the joke as being in the 'New York style', where the comedy comes not from the joke itself but from its inappropriateness and extremity. There's no doubt Trump's comment was jaw-droppingly blunt and disrespectful. But *that's* the joke. It's hardly a presidential way of talking.

Candidates are also normally so risk averse, and so worried about causing any kind of offence to potential voters, that they seek to be as bland as possible in their speech. Trump was not shackled by this desire to play it safe. On the campaign trail, he was happy to offend and enrage people who would probably never vote for him anyway, and delight others in the process. It ensured he got all the press attention, and all the other Republican candidates found themselves starved of coverage.

This way of talking and joking, Adams argues, is completely alien to those on the West Coast of the USA, where people tend to be far more agreeable and concerned for one another's feelings. Trump, as a New Yorker, is much more comfortable with conflict and controversy.

It is not for me, a Brit who's only spent one week in Manhattan, to wholeheartedly agree with Adams, but it is clear that Trump was trying to be funny when he made the joke at McCain's expense. One might say it's a meta-joke, one step removed from the joke itself.

---

[4] The three-times-married Trump attending a Family Leadership Summit in Iowa is already an amusingly incongruous situation but that's not the joke.

It's catching on

This kind of comedy sounds obscure but it's not unusual. You will see it in popular TV shows like *Family Guy* that often revel in the extremity of a joke. *Family Guy* is an animated show about the Griffin family from Rhode Island, not far from New York. It was created by Seth MacFarlane, who is from Kent, Connecticut, which is also not far from New York. Scott Adams is on to something.

MacFarlane was able to use the animated family sitcom setting, already well established by *The Simpsons*, and take it further. The show makes the jokes often very caustic and sometimes laboured for comic effect. The result is that they can be shocking, which would take us back to the surprise–shock idea in Part 1. But the shock *is* the joke. The joke might not be the words themselves, but that they are being said in such an outlandish setting or in such a heavy-handed or repetitive way.

Sometimes, a joke which isn't all that funny is laboured for a very long time. For example, there is a scene in which the characters take an emetic to make them vomit, which they then do for an uncomfortably long time. It's repellent, but that's the joke.

In another episode, there is a fight scene between Peter Griffin, one of the main characters, and a man dressed as a chicken that goes on and on and on, lasting nearly two minutes. The chicken man returns in future episodes with escalating scenes of absurd cartoon violence.

On another occasion, Peter takes an absurdly long time trying to throw a dead frog out of a window without touching it. In that case, the joke is that a fast-paced animated TV show should spend such a long time showing us something we would not normally see in such detail. It's a meta-joke.

Getting it

The problem is that laughing at meta-jokes can place you in an extremely difficult position. It looks really bad. Let's go back to the Trump joke about McCain. If you'd been there and laughed out loud, some might have turned to you and thought less of you. It would appear that you were enjoying Trump's disrespect of a valiant war hero. In actual fact, you were laughing at the inappropriate extremity of Trump's joke. *But the laugh sounds the same.* The offended McCain supporters might not have realized you were laughing at the crassness of Trump's humour, rather than the heroism of a war veteran.

Laughing at meta-jokes can place you at risk of ostracism. It may cost you friends, or a job. Or land you in court. That's where we are heading with the next chapter.

23

Springtime for pug dogs

One of my favourite movies of all time is *Indiana Jones and the Last Crusade*. Perhaps it's because it was 1989 and I was 14. I've always loved Harrison Ford's lone hero persona. Everything is up to him. If he doesn't get it done, it won't get done. This is encapsulated at the start of *The Last Crusade* when the young Indy is separated from his troop of Scouts. He is all alone and concludes, 'Everybody's lost but me.' It's a good joke.

When Indy grows up, he has enemies: Nazis. When he sees them for the first time in *The Last Crusade*, busying themselves pushing counters around maps with long poles the way they do in movies, Indy mutters to himself, 'Nazis. I hate these guys.'

Nazis are the action-movie director's greatest friend. They have fantastic, distinctive uniforms, some of which even have skulls on them.[1] Nazis are fanatically devoted to their cause, and their Führer. And they have really good, well-engineered kit. The most important thing is this: our hero can kill as many of them as you like and still be a goodie. You would have to go a long way to invent better baddies than Nazis.

Harrison Ford was doubly blessed in this regard. As Indiana Jones, he got to shoot Nazis. In *Star Wars*, he was able to blast away as many Storm Troopers as he liked as well. And let's be

---

[1] See the sketch on this subject in Series 1, Episode 1 of *That Mitchell and Webb Look*, in which an SS soldier realizes that, despite the Nazi propaganda, he might in fact be the baddie.

honest: Storm Troopers are Nazis. Even the name is a bit of a lift. Storm Troopers, or *Sturmtruppen,* were German shock troops in the First World War.

In today's common parlance, Nazis are still the embodiment of evil. They are the worst people possible. Perhaps the worst imaginable when one considers the mechanization of mass slaughter that they masterminded.[2]

It belongs in a museum

At the time, Indiana Jones could not have known what the Nazis would be capable of. The first three films are set before the Second World War and so his actions against German soldiers are not entirely justified. To Indy, the worst thing about the Nazis is that they are terrible archaeologists, plundering relics that 'belong in a museum'. They are attempting to co-opt the Ark of the Covenant and the Holy Grail to manipulate the power of God, in whom Indy scarcely believes.

But who cares about the details and the timelines? We can take what we know now and superimpose it on the Nazis of the 1930s. Cinematically, it works. All is well. We don't watch films rationally. We watch them emotionally.

Common sense and cool-headedness are often thrown out of the window when we encounter moving pictures. This includes YouTube videos like the one made by Count Dankula. So what did he do?

A dog called Buddha

Count Dankula, the avatar of Mark Meechan from Lanarkshire in Scotland, decided to annoy his girlfriend by making a video about her sweet little pug dog called Buddha. What's the most offensive, least cute thing a pug dog called Buddha can do? A Nazi

---

[2] If you've not seen *Conspiracy* (2001) on the chillingly civilized way in which the Final Solution was devised and imposed, I highly recommend it.

salute whenever someone says '*Sieg heil*'. So that's what he did. He trained Buddha to do just that. He made a three-minute video of the fruits of his labour and put it on YouTube in 2016.

What makes the video especially unpalatable is his continual attempts to get a response from the dog by saying 'Gas the Jews.' Defenders of Dankula might argue that this is a meta-joke, since anti-Semitism is so unacceptable that saying such an offensive phrase is funny. But the main joke is that his girlfriend has been pranked and her adorable dog has been ruined in the most extreme way possible.

In 2017, Meechan was arrested for this video and appeared at Airdrie Sheriff Court. He was charged with perpetrating a hate crime under Section 127 of the Communications Act 2003. We'll come to whether that is or is not a good law later, but what had Meechan–Dankula actually done?

One could argue that he had only done what Steven Spielberg and hundreds of other movie directors have done in action movies. He co-opted Nazism for its embodiment of wickedness in order to make a piece of entertainment. Spielberg grabbed the Nazis to make a movie about an archaeological hero. Dankula grabbed the Nazis to make a sick joke at the expense of the girlfriend and her dog, Buddha.

Fellow Youtuber Felix 'PewDiePie' Kjellberg, who had lucrative links with Google and Disney, did something similar in 2017. As part of a joke to show 'how crazy the modern world is, specifically some of the services available online', PewDiePie paid two Indian men five dollars to hold up a sign which contained the words 'Death to All Jews'.[3] Many failed to see the joke. Arwa Mahdawi, writing in *The Guardian*'s 'Comment Is Free' column, was among them. She wrote:

---

[3] There is a lovely irony here. In looking up PewDiePie videos on YouTube, I was immediately confronted with an automatically generated advert – for Fiverr, the kind of website PewDiePie was satirizing with his controversial video.

A joke is never just a joke, you see: it always has consequences. Jokes help identify and solidify social divisions. You either get the joke and you're one of us, or you don't get it and you're one of them. Jokes also help normalize unpalatable ideas. And, unconscious though it may have been, PewDiePie has already helped do just that: helped antisemitism become just a little bit more mainstream.[4]

Indy meets the Führer

But where does this end? One could argue – although I'm not sure I would – that Spielberg is doing something similar in the *Indiana Jones* movies. In *The Last Crusade*, Indiana Jones finds himself at a Nazi rally in which books are being burned. Disguised as a German soldier and holding a book which contains key secrets about the Holy Grail, Indy is buffeted into the Führer's path by a surging crowd. He ends up being face to face with Adolf Hitler himself. They both look at the book in Indiana's hand. Everything stops. Hitler holds out a hand and a minion hands him a pencil. Hitler signs his autograph in the book and moves on. Is this making light of the most evil man of the twentieth century? Did it help Nazism 'become just a little bit more mainstream'?

What is the difference between Indy's comic encounter with Hitler and the short-lived sitcom *Heil Honey I'm Home!*? Adolf Hitler and his wife Eva live next door to the Goldensteins. With hilarious consequences. The programme was commissioned by BSB in 1990 (before it merged with Sky).

Again, the joke is not really about Nazism. There was a caption card at the beginning explaining that *Heil Honey I'm Home!* was a long-lost US sitcom recently rediscovered in some archives in Burbank, California.[5] The joke is that in the 1950s and 1960s,

---

[4] <www.theguardian.com/commentisfree/2017/feb/15/youtube-pewdiepie-thinks-death-to-all-jews-joke-laughing-yet>.

[5] <https://web.archive.org/web/20070404125429/http://www.bbc.co.uk/comedy/guide/articles/h/heilhoneyimhome__1299003509.shtml>.

the Americans were used to turning any domestic situation into a sitcom. Hitler was being used to create the worst possible domestic sitcom imaginable.

The show was cancelled after one episode. Artistically this might have been a mercy, since the idea sounds more like a three-minute sketch than six half-hour episodes when the joke might run a little thin.

The Producers

The makers of *Heil Honey I'm Home!* might have been mystified that they were cut so short given the lengthy career of Mel Brooks, who portrayed Hitler himself many times and wrote numerous sketches about him, such as 'Hitler on Ice' from the movie *History of the World Part 1*.

Brooks' biggest hit, however, must surely be *The Producers*, originally a film from 1967 starring Zero Mostel and Gene Wilder. It was remade as a stage musical in 2001, starring Nathan Lane and Matthew Broderick. This musical version was in turn shot as a new movie in 2005. What is the premise of the story?

Thanks to a timid accountant, a dishonest, washed-up Broadway producer realizes he can make more money with a flop that closes on the first night than he can with a hit. Therefore, he needs a show that will have to close immediately.

The two trawl though script after script before they find the perfect show: *Springtime for Hitler: A Gay Romp with Adolf and Eva at Berchtesgaden*. The producer says that it's virtually 'a love letter to Hitler'. The play is written by deranged ex-Nazi Franz Liebkind.[6]

The play is given to the campest and worst director on Broadway, Roger De Bris, and it is rehearsed and presented to an

---

[6] This is an unusually subtle joke as Liebkind means 'lovechild', a bastard. I have only just noticed this despite having seen the West End version of the show once and the movies many times over many years.

audience who are initially open-mouthed. A few storm out, saying it's in bad taste. This is, of course, true. It is. That is the point on many levels. The remaining audience see the outlandish portrayal of Hitler and mistake it for a goofy satire, finding it hilariously funny. The show is a smash hit, a catastrophe for the producers, who go to jail for fraud.

In short, *The Producers* portrays a character using Nazism as a convenient shorthand for something offensive that is guaranteed to produce a negative reaction. In their videos, Count Dankula and PewDiePie did essentially the same thing. Dankula was arrested, tried and prosecuted for a hate crime. PewDiePie found his links with Disney and Google were severed, possibly costing millions in lost advertising revenue. Mel Brooks won 12 Tony Awards. In one awards speech he publicly thanked Hitler. Even Dankula could not expect to get away with that. Why is that?

Who's who?

As we saw in Part 1 of this book, the actual joke is only part of the story. There is a wider context here which includes the identity of the joker. One cannot help but notice that Mel Brooks is at least two things that Dankula is not.

First, Brooks is a highly respected comedian with a long career and proven track record in comedy. Not only is *The Producers* on his CV, but also *The Young Frankenstein, Space Balls, History of the World Part 1* and *Blazing Saddles* (but let's not get into that last one right now). Before that he was a writer for numerous hit TV shows. Mel Brooks is a comedy institution.

Dankula is not in that class and does not claim to be. On his Twitter profile, he describes himself as a 'professional shitposter'. This seems a fair description. He's an internet contrarian who pushes the limits of free speech and says anti-social things purely because he can.

Moreover, some people who rushed to his defence are not held in high regard in polite company. While high-profile comedians like Ricky Gervais and David Baddiel were vocal in their criticism of the court's decision, there was also strong support from Tommy Robinson, formerly of the controversial anti-immigrant English Defence League. Robinson created certain associations in the minds of those looking at Dankula's case. Regardless of the law and his credible supporters, Dankula was never going to create a good impression in the media or in court.

The second pertinent difference between Dankula and Brooks is that the latter is Jewish. Should that matter? Maybe it shouldn't, but it does. It matters because when Brooks portrays camp goose-stepping Nazis and comic versions of Hitler, it is not credible to say that he is secretly in sympathy with Jew-murdering fascists. Some may find Brooks' comedy to be in poor taste, as some friends of mine did when they went to see *The Producers*, partly on my recommendation. But they did not come away feeling they had been to a covert Nazi rally or recruitment drive.[7]

'The Limo'

Being Jewish, in this case, obviously puts one at an advantage when covering material that, in the wrong hands, could be open to the charge of appearing to normalize anti-Semitism. Jerry Seinfeld took full advantage in Series 3, Episode 18 of his eponymous sitcom in an episode entitled 'The Limo'. Jerry and his friend George return from the airport in a limousine that has been sent for a man called O'Brien. Jerry saw O'Brien unable to get on his plane and knows that he will not be claiming this limo. So George, pretending to be O'Brien and Jerry his friend Murphy, takes it. It is only on the journey that they discover that O'Brien is a high-profile neo-Nazi and Hitler admirer who is going to give a

---

[7] Brooks' comedies about Nazis are not always so brash. In 1983, he produced a remake of a 1942 film *To Be or Not To Be*, combining slapstick comedy with some raw emotion about the crimes of the Nazi regime in Poland.

speech at a rally. This is all especially funny since George and Jerry are both Jewish.

Given it is Jerry Seinfeld's show, there is no question of his attempting to normalize, or give a voice to, anti-Semitism. Neither is Spielberg, the maker of *Schindler's List*, going to be credibly accused of the same thing for his levity about Hitler in *The Last Crusade*.

An odious criminal act

Count Dankula is not Jewish. His prosecutors in court were able to suggest that Dankula's video was 'an odious criminal act that was dressed up to look like a joke'. His motives were mixed, they argued, or *could credibly be construed as such*. Therefore, he must be found guilty. The sheriff agreed. I do not. Here's what I think, in case you're wondering.

I would happily concede that the joke was misjudged and abhorrent. Technically, it works as a joke, given the incongruity with the pug dog called Buddha – and that the intensity and insensitivity of the language is totally disproportionate. It's not a joke I would do. But that doesn't mean that he should not have done it, although I do think less of him for having done so. I also suspect he is uninterested in my opinion of him.

I would have no problem with YouTube, as the host of the video, taking it down since they are a private company (although they are often unclear on their rules and apply them inconsistently). Similarly, Disney and Google were within their rights to sever their links with PewDiePie, even though they should have realized what they were signing up to when they made a deal with him in the first place.

I think the Communications Act of 2003 is a bad law. It is worrying that the only proof required for a conviction is not demonstrable harm, or even clear intent, but the possibility of a joke 'being construed' as offensive. Many jokes with clearly noble or harmless intentions could be worthy of a guilty verdict.

Many have applauded the prosecution of contrarian Dankula, but may yet live to see this law enacted against people they like and respect. Or it may be used against them themselves if a joke they have made on Twitter in the past is suddenly branded hate speech.

Some said that Dankula should have known better. The *Charlie Hebdo* case highlights why this an unhelpful comment in the wider context.

Je ne suis pas Charlie

When two gunmen killed 12 people and injured another 11 at the offices of *Charlie Hebdo* in Paris in broad daylight for jokes about Islam's prophet, the world was horrified and appalled. The phrase '*Je suis Charlie*' circulated the internet and found its way on to placards and t-shirts, as a mark of solidarity for the dead.

President François Hollande called the shootings a 'terrorist attack of the most extreme barbarity', describing those who had been killed as 'heroes'.[8] He declared a day of national mourning. World leaders turned out.

But soon, other comments began to emerge, questioning the wisdom of *Charlie Hebdo*'s targeting of Islam. In 2012, after another controversial incident, White House Press Secretary Jay Carney told reporters,

> We are aware that a French magazine published cartoons featuring a figure resembling the Prophet Muhammad, and obviously we have questions about the judgment of publishing something like this . . . We don't question the right of something like this to be published, we just question the judgment behind the decision to publish it.[9]

---

[8] '1 of 3 Suspects in Paris Shootings Surrenders', Voice of America, 7 January 2015.

[9] White House briefing, 20 September 2012.

What is the use of having the right to do something if there will never be a time when that right can be exercised? Does this not go at least some way to condoning the inexcusable murder of those who make jokes we do not like? Surely the right to free speech must be defended? In his preface to *Animal Farm*, George Orwell wrote, 'If liberty means anything at all it means the right to tell people what they do not want to hear.' These words are now inscribed on the wall of the BBC's New Broadcasting House next to a statue of Orwell.

It is difficult to defend free speech, including jokes in poor taste or considered blasphemous, without at least looking as though you partly agree with the joke or find it funny. This is why many do not bother. No one would choose Dankula to be the poster boy for free speech. Rights and freedoms are eroded. The result is politicians rush in with vague laws like the Communications Act 2003. Even if the law were less vague, I would still argue that all Dankula has done is the well-worn comedy trick of grabbing the Nazi trope as many have done before him and will continue to do in the future. He's done it crudely and unpleasantly, but should that be a crime? I don't think so.

24

Jerry! Jerry! Jerry!

B ritish Christians are not prone to protesting with placards or taking legal action about jokes. Quiet grumbling, tuts of disappointment and comments that 'they wouldn't do jokes about Islam' are the preferred responses (see Part 2). In 2005, however, modest but meaningful crowds assembled outside BBC offices in London, Birmingham, Belfast and Cardiff. This was covered on the BBC news bulletins and their website. Even opponents of the BBC have to admit that the corporation is excellent at broadcasting criticism of itself.

The situation escalated. Fifty thousand complaints were received, partly because of an orchestrated campaign by Christian Voice, a lobby group headed by Stephen Green which took legal action against the Corporation.

The reason for the brouhaha was the BBC's decision to broadcast *Jerry Springer: The Opera*, a controversial production that blended *The Jerry Springer Show* with Faust for comical and satirical effect.

It is a fundamentally brilliant idea. *The Jerry Springer Show*, which peaked in the late 1990s, traded in dysfunctional family relationships which, the producers hoped, would descend into barely restrained violence. It's a superb starting point for a comic opera, abundant with emotionally charged scenes and loud expressions of horror, regret and repentance.

The show began life as a one-act fringe show for a cast of two, written by Richard Thomas and tested at Battersea Arts Centre in

2000. Comedian and director Stewart Lee became involved, and by April 2003 it was a three-act production at the National Theatre with a cast of 33. Michael Brandon (*Dempsey and Makepeace*) starred as Jerry Springer. In November, it transferred to the West End and ran until 2005, winning all four 'Best Musical' awards.[1] The show toured the UK, but dates were affected by threats of protests. A Broadway production was talked about but never materialized.

The demand of art

Before we launch into the rights and wrongs of the jokes and consider whether Christians were right to take offence and wave placards, let us take a moment to consider roughly what happens in the show. This is an important part of the process, and one which the reasonable reader would consider to be rather basic. But it is often overlooked in the rush for comment, opinion and headlines.

Even a summary of the show is not adequate. It is very hard to argue that any art can be evaluated without experiencing it as the artist intended. In his brilliant book, *An Experiment in Criticism*, C. S. Lewis observes:

> The first demand any work of art makes upon us is surrender. Look. Listen. Receive. Get yourself out of the way. (There is no good asking first whether the work before you deserves such a surrender, for until you have surrendered you cannot possibly find out.)[2]

This seems entirely reasonable. Beleaguered parents use a similar technique on small children in trying to introduce them to new foods, arguing, 'How do you know you don't like it when you haven't even tried it?'

---

[1] What this also tells you is that there are probably too many awards ceremonies for West End shows.

[2] C. S. Lewis, *An Experiment in Criticism* (Cambridge: University of Cambridge Press, 1961), p. 19.

But the devout Christian may riposte with a verse from the Bible written by St Peter in his first epistle: 'Be sober-minded; be watchful. Your adversary the devil prowls around like a roaring lion, seeking someone to devour' (1 Peter 5.8). There are many other verses about purity and fleeing temptation as we saw in Part 2, the 'Philippians 4 manoeuvre' in action.

There is some validity to this argument, since one does not need to watch pornographic films, for example, in order to oppose them on principle. But then no one is seriously claiming pornography is an art that requires careful viewing or deep consideration. Surrender would clearly be unwise. *Jerry Springer: The Opera* undoubtedly has artistic merit and so the 'I don't need to see it to know it's all wrong' argument is not appropriate here. A Christian may feel that he or she cannot, in all conscience, see it, but should admit that his or her criticism of the work is severely impaired.

A brief detour into Westeros

A more recent example of a problematic work has surfaced in the form of *Game of Thrones*. The show is controversial for its use of nudity as well as graphic, wanton violence. An influential Christian pastor, Kevin DeYoung, argued that he found it hard to understand why Christians were watching this programme. Reading his blog post on the Gospel Coalition website, we get a sense of the 'I don't need to watch it to know it's wrong' argument. DeYoung writes:

> True, I haven't seen it. Not an episode. Not a scene. I hardly know anything about the show. I know many people consider it absolutely riveting – full of compelling characters, an engrossing story, and excellent acting, writing, and aesthetics.
>
> But isn't it also full of sex? Like lots and lots of incredibly graphic sex? I did a Google search for 'Game of Thrones sex' and found headlines (I avoided images and only read

headlines) about sex scenes you can't unsee and the best sex scenes of the series and why *Game of Thrones* is so committed to nudity and explicit (sometimes violent) sex.[3]

His ability to comment on the work having not seen it is not entirely invalidated, but makes it hard to take his opinion seriously. I have seen every episode of *Game of Thrones*, and, while enjoying it, have found some scenes very troubling and offensive. This is partly the intention of the writers and producers of the show. The sexual violence is unpleasant viewing. No one making the show is commending such behaviour. Its very portrayal is a refutation of it. The show also portrays incest, as does the Bible, along with dire warnings about such behaviour.

DeYoung has clearly attempted to research the show without watching it or viewing a single image. On the one hand, this is a laudable attempt to keep himself from seeing sexual imagery that he cannot 'unsee' and not be bitten on the leg by the prowling lion and then consumed entirely. But such an approach inhibits his ability to comment on the show.

His hand is shown when he undermines his stern argument by writing, 'But isn't it also full of sex?' The answer to this is 'no'. It is not *full* of sex. There is sexual imagery and some of it far too explicit for my taste and sensibilities, but one cannot really say it is 'full of sex'.

I sympathize with DeYoung's concerns about the show and his desire to write hyperbolically, hence 'full of sex'. I believe he is right to challenge his fellow Christians to think twice before losing themselves in the fictional world of George R. R. Martin's Westeros. But DeYoung's understandable refusal to 'surrender. Look. Listen. Receive', as C. S. Lewis suggests, severely compromises his critique.

---

[3] <www.thegospelcoalition.org/blogs/kevin-deyoung/i-dont-understand-christians-watching-game-of-thrones/>.

Advanced joking

Hitting pockets

It would be very frustrating to have your work attacked and boy-
cotted when those complaining make a point of refusing to watch
it, especially when this is costing you a great deal of money in
legal bills and lost revenue. Stewart Lee, the director and co-writer
of *Jerry Springer: The Opera*, wrote in *The Guardian* that the complaints had cost him a lot of money. Royalties had to be waived in
order to make the UK tour of the show financially viable. A major
frustration, though, was a lack of engagement with the work itself
from people who should know better. He wrote:

> a bedraggled protestor hands me a leaflet complaining that
> the show calls God 'the fascist tyrant on high'. The line appears
> in the show on a note written by Satan and is derived from
> Milton's *Paradise Lost*. Have any of these protesters actually
> seen the opera?[4]

If you wish to view the production for yourself and make up your
own mind, you can. The DVD is still available. Lots of copies
were left unsold when some large retailers like Sainsbury's and
Woolworth's refused to stock it after receiving a number of complaints from their customers.

Were Christians right to insist their retailers withdraw this
DVD from sale? They were, of course, within their legal rights to
ask, but was it wise? The DVD sales were, to some extent, the end
game. For now, let us engage with the actual content of the show,
rather than reacting to the headlines about the swearwords and
the alleged blasphemy.

What actually happens?

Act I is a 'normal' but exaggerated episode of *The Jerry Springer
Show*. One guest, Dwight, is cheating on his partner with a lady
called Zandra as well as a transsexual, Tremont. Another guest,

---

[4] <www.theguardian.com/stage/2006/feb/15/theatre2>.

Montel, tells his partner, Andrea, that he likes to dress as a baby and that he is cheating on her with Baby Jane, a woman who dresses as a little girl. Jerry's warm-up man becomes involved and is fired. The final guests are a frustrated stripper and a member of the Ku Klux Klan, whose fellow Klan members rush the stage. A gun is produced and Jerry is accidentally shot. End of Act I.

Act II finds Jerry in Purgatory trying to justify himself to the ghosts of his talk show guests, who have all suffered horrible fates. The warm-up man from Act I is revealed to be Satan himself. Baby Jane intervenes to ask Satan to spare Jerry's soul. He decides to force Jerry to do a special show with him in Hell. End of Act II.

Act III takes place in a charred, hellish version of the real TV studio. Satan wants an apology for his expulsion from heaven and some kind of showdown with Jesus, who resembles Montel from Act I. Jesus and Satan trade accusations, as do Adam and Eve, arguing like guests from Act I. The Virgin Mary arrives and chaos ensues. Jerry hopes for a miracle. He gets one when God and the angels turn up. They fight over Jerry with Satan's devils. Jerry eventually finds himself suspended over a flaming pit and is forced to be honest with himself and the audience. He wakes up in his own television studio, having been shot, cradled in a security guard's arms, in time to give his final thought.

All of the above is sung. It's an opera. It is done with a brash, crass tone not dissimilar from the work of Parker and Stone (*South Park, Team America: World Police*). There is plenty of profane language. Newspapers ran stories that there were a reported 8,000 obscenities, although Lee states there are 174. But what's the show *really* about?

What's the joke?

Many argued that *Jerry Springer: The Opera* was a vicious and blasphemous attack on Christianity without having seen the show, making constructive discussion of the work impossible. When it was broadcast, over 50,000 complaints were received by the BBC, over 84 per cent of which arrived before the show was actually transmitted at 10 p.m.[5] This is ironic since the opera is satirizing the original *Jerry Springer Show* for being the very epitome of idiotic television, pitting uninformed and offended parties against each other, hoping it will lead to on-screen violence. The show, then, is partly prophetic, in critiquing society's inability to discuss contentious issues rationally, calmly and with respect.

The show clearly has themes relating to Milton's *Paradise Lost* and the ejection of Satan from God's divine council, which is hinted at in the Bible but rarely made explicit. Given that this theological story does not take place in the first act of the show, it seems unconvincing to argue that it is the main target or overriding theme of the show.

The Satan–God clash works well as the ultimate test of Jerry's skills as a mediator between warring families, while being an intense moral examination for him. One could argue it is a plot device that almost overpowers the original theme because of its intensity and controversy – in the same way that *Springtime for Hitler* dominates *The Producers*.

The media were not interested in the nuances of the show. Christian Voice's Stephen Green found himself to be at the forefront of the campaign against the show. Radio stations and rolling news programmes with hours to fill were only too happy to give a platform to those with a clear, simple viewpoint that can be expressed forcefully and without nuance.

Blasphemy

The press preferred to suggest the show contained thousands of swearwords, and claimed that Jesus appeared as a nappy-wearing sexual deviant. In *The Guardian*, Lee wrote, 'Jesus isn't in a nappy. OK?' which is technically true. But the show is inviting the viewer to draw clear parallels between characters in Acts I, II and III. The

---

[5] <www.bbc.co.uk/complaints/pdf/apps_springer.pdf>.

actor playing nappy-wearing Montel in Act I also portrays Jesus in Act III. One may conclude that the writers of the show were being wilfully blasphemous.

Mark Thompson, Director-General of the BBC at the time and a practising Christian, disagreed. He said that 'There is nothing in this which I believe to be blasphemous.' Thompson's fellow Christians might have been rather puzzled at such a statement. Is there really *nothing* blasphemous in the show? The Christian would define blasphemy as taking the Lord's name in vain, pointing to one of the Ten Commandments, as found in Exodus 20.7 and Deuteronomy 5.11.

But what does it mean to take the Lord's name in vain? The show's creators would argue that they have done nothing of the sort. They have used the names of God, Jesus and Mary carefully and intentionally. The divine family represents a coherent codified moral and theological system to test the character of Jerry Springer. *He* is the one on trial, not God. The show could be described as an examination of the culture of the late 1990s, in which Jerry Springer became a very rich man for hosting a television show which encouraged voyeurism and had serious consequences in the lives of those who took part.

Job description

Mark Thompson may point to the first few chapters of Job to attempt to justify his statement. In those chapters, a rich and powerful man is put on trial by a divine council, albeit in his absence. The Bible frequently portrays characters, even heroes of the Christian faith, bowing down to idols or doing terrible things in God's name. The events, as described, may be blasphemous, but to call the Bible itself blasphemous is patently absurd.

Thompson could have plausibly said he believed the show used biblical themes and imagery that many Christians would find offensive, but that overall the play itself was not blasphemous. But his statement that 'there is nothing in this which I believe to be blasphemous' is much harder to justify since words are put into the mouths of divine characters that are clearly offensive in context. Either way, Thompson's assurances did not convincingly allay the fears of other Christians.

Stewart Lee was not concerned about the sin of blasphemy, being a public atheist. He does not fear divine reprisals. But what about legal ones? At the time, blasphemy was still a crime and Christian Voice took the producers of the show to court. Was that wise and did it work? And what is the legal situation now? If we look, we will find that it is now Christianity that is more likely to be placed in the dock.

25

Jerry and the lawmakers

There are many ways to express an opinion. Some people
wrap themselves in the flag. Others burn it. But the majority
of us silently regard it as an emblem of the freedom to express
ourselves as we see fit. In dancing, there are many ways to express
oneself, ways that the rest of us do not always regard as 'our way'.
Some put on a pair of tights and perform classical ballet. Others
attire themselves in fancy dress and promenade on a ballroom
floor. Jimmy Lee Laedeke dons a Groucho Marx bikini and two
G-strings and prances before the patrons of The Club Carlin.[1]

These words were uttered in the case of the city of Billings
vs Jimmy Lee Laedeke, heard in the Supreme Court
of Montana in 1991. It concerned a burlesque dancer,
Laedeke, who was accused of breaking a number of laws, including an obscure state law that if you start performing a song on
stage, you are committed to finishing it.

Lists of redundant or strange American state laws abound on
the internet, and we all giggle at the folly of laws about greased
pigs, yard sales, honking car horns and licking toads. Such laws
were not passed by madmen but a rational state legislators facing
problems different from those of today.

The way we feel about the morality or legality of certain actions
can change very rapidly. Attitudes to same-sex relationships have

---

[1] <www.courtlistener.com/opinion/882237/city-of-billings-v-laedeke/>.

changed quickly in the UK in the past 15 years. Even when the Civil Partnership Act, granting same-sex couples legal rights, was given royal assent in November 2004, there was little prospect of, or demand for, same-sex marriage. But a law providing for this rapidly followed, and retrospectively seems inevitable. The discussion around sexual politics now looks very different from when *Jerry Springer: The Opera* was being broadcast on BBC2 on 8 January 2005.

The letter of the law

Laws against blasphemy in the UK were abolished in the Criminal Justice and Immigration Act in 2008,[2] so were still in force at the time of the *Jerry Springer: The Opera* controversy. One of the larger bones of contention, possibly the femur, was a line in which the Jesus character said that sometimes he felt 'a bit gay'. In 2005, ascribing homosexual feelings to Christ was more shocking than doing so in 2019. However, amid all the complaints about the show, this had some legal resonance with the last successful prosecution for blasphemy in the UK decades earlier.

'The Love that Dares to Speak its Name' was a poem by James Kirkup published in *Gay News* on 3 June 1976. The poem was written from the viewpoint of a Roman centurion who witnessed the crucifixion of Christ, and describes him having sexual intercourse with Jesus, claiming that Jesus had had sex with many other men from the Gospel accounts, including Pontius Pilate.

Mary Whitehouse was so appalled at the poem that she launched a private prosecution against *Gay News* on the grounds of blasphemous libel, a common law offence (based on precedent rather than specific statutes). She was successful. *Gay News* and Denis Lemon, the publisher, were fined and ordered to pay costs. A suspended prison sentence was also issued, but this was overturned on appeal, even though the House of Lords upheld the conviction.

---

[2] Northern Ireland remains an exception to this.

Stephen Green of Christian Voice attempted to do the same with *Jerry Springer: The Opera*. He brought a private blasphemy prosecution against the BBC. But the charges were rejected by the City of Westminster Magistrates' Court and the High Court rejected the appeal. The reason given seems a little arbitrary: common law blasphemy offences specifically did not apply to stage productions or broadcast programmes.[3] Even if this were not the case, the court said, there was no case to answer, because even if the play contained scenes deeply offensive to some Christians, the play's target was Jerry Springer's television show, not Christianity.[4]

The BBC was naturally delighted at the decision, issuing a statement which said, 'We believe the work, taken in its proper context, satirizes and attacks exploitative chat shows and not the Christian religion.' This is a fair assessment of the work, but it assumes the ends justify the means. If the show commits blasphemy in the process of satirizing a TV format, is it not still an offence?

Law changes

The point is moot since the law is no longer in force. New laws, which resulted in the prosecution of Count Dankula, are attempting to do very different things from the old common laws. Previously, the Christian faith had a privileged status because Christianity had historically been dominant in the United Kingdom, as we saw in Part 2 (Chapter 18). Now the law is rapidly becoming a problem for Christianity in the UK, with Christians being arrested and prosecuted, rather than blasphemers.

Although some forms of Christianity have declined over the previous decades, there has been no great desire to dismantle the apparatus of Christendom and sweep away the faith entirely,

---

[3] Under Section 2(4) of the Theatres Act 1968 and Section 6 of the Broadcasting Act 1990. Since you ask.

[4] <https://uk.practicallaw.thomsonreuters.com/6-379-8525>.

other than by a number of secularists and atheists, who are vocal but small in number. But the changes to the law, and what they are seeking to achieve, have had unintended consequences.

The decline in church attendance, the rise of secularism and the influx of immigrants with different faiths have caused lawmakers to believe that no one single faith could or should be given special treatment or a protected legal status. This is puzzling given the entrenchment of Christianity in the power structures of the UK, setting in motion legal clashes in the future.

Moreover, if the new laws are meant to be protecting *all* faiths, what is the moral or philosophical basis for these new laws? If our society does not base its law on the Judeo-Christian faith or a clearly defined alternative, like Islam, how does it regulate speech and expression and jokes? What becomes the measure of behaviour or speech that cannot be tolerated? Offence. Uh oh.

We have already seen that offence is a poor yardstick for working out whether something should or should not have been said or done. It is an entirely subjective measure of harm. Anyone can say they were offended, and there is no clear way of proving whether or not they were, even if we do believe this is a valid criterion for the law.

Lawmakers might argue that the main aim of their laws has been attempting to protect people, especially preventing young people being radicalized by religious fundamentalists who seek to do harm. The resulting laws, like Section 127 of the Communications Act 2003, end up being vague, confusing and open to wide interpretation, as we saw with the case against Count Dankula.

Connor Griffiths, Deputy Editor of online journal *Keep Calm and Talk Law*, writes:

It may be tempting to look at the fact that Meechan was only sentenced to pay an £800 fine and think that, all things considered, everything turned out okay. This should not be the case: a precedent has now been set that allows the courts and CPS [Crown Prosecution Service] to challenge and criminalise comedy and free speech through the use of an unnecessary, ill-fitting and outdated law.

Section 127 of the CA 2003 needs serious reconsideration by Parliament. Whether someone faces prison time should not be dependent on the sensitivities of a random person on the internet. The restriction of offensive content leads to unacceptable uncertainty: the CPS is able to pick and choose which content it deems criminally offensive and which it doesn't.[5]

While the old blasphemy laws may have been anachronistic or anomalous, the new laws are, at best, unworkable and contradictory. Most likely, they are open to abuse or applied at the whim of the Crown Prosecution Service. At worst, they are tyrannical.

Manic street preachers

But the law is not just a problem for self-confessed 'shitposters' like Mark Meechan–Count Dankula. There are numerous stories every year of Christian street preachers being arrested for reading out verses of the Bible which are perceived to be homophobic.

Mike Overd, for example, was detained in a shopping area in Bridgwater on Saturday 19 August 2017 'on suspicion of a racially or religiously-motivated public order offence'.[6] He was released without charge, but had only recently appealed successfully against a public order conviction. Leon Da Silva claimed Overd told him that he was going to hell for being a homosexual. Offended by Overd's comments, Da Silva launched a petition calling on Somerset County Council to ban Overd from preaching in Bridgwater and the county town of Taunton nearby.

---

[5] <www.keepcalmtalklaw.co.uk/offensive-jokes-becoming-criminal-count-dankulas-conviction/>.

[6] <www.premier.org.uk/News/UK/Street-preacher-arrested-again>.

Advanced joking

Overd wasn't telling jokes but expressing a theological opinion. The effect is the same. It's a good example of the profound shift in the law and what our society holds dear. Previously, the law had protected the name and honour of Jesus Christ, in whose name Overd would argue he was speaking. Now it protects the honour of the people offended by this message – in this case, Leon Da Silva.

In the comparatively short time since *Jerry Springer: The Opera* was performed and broadcast, social attitudes and the law have changed to the point where a conservative Christian is now far more likely to be arrested than a blasphemer. Is this progress? Some would say it is, including those Christians who find the more conservative strand of the Church distasteful, offensive or just plain wrong.

So where do we go from here? What kind of laws do we want? Is it desirable that we lock up people who make jokes that people might find offensive? Or does anything go? In some countries, blasphemy is punished by death, so prison would be an improvement. Most comedians are familiar with the concept of 'dying' on stage, which is bad enough. But being executed? Tough crowd.

26

Careful now

The British are not good at complaining. Sometimes, when really riled, we might manage a cough and 'Now, look here', but you can still be sure of one thing. We will ultimately end up apologizing for causing a fuss.

This self-awareness and hand-wringing is now acknowledged in our public demonstrations. Quite often, you will see placards being waved that are comically understated, like 'THIS IS ALL TERRIBLY UPSETTING' when President Trump arrived in the UK in July 2018 amid protests. One often sees a sign which says, 'Down with this sort of thing'. This is a reference to an episode of the sitcom *Father Ted*[1] in which Fathers Ted and Dougal protest against a blasphemous movie called *The Passion of Saint Tibulus*. They hold up two signs. One says, 'Down with this sort of thing'. The other says, 'Careful now'.

When we see protests about blasphemous movies or jokes in cities like Tehran, we see a very different picture. There is no room for apology or self-referential whimsy. It is full-scale, weapons-grade indignation and rage. TV news programmes never tire of showing anti-Western radicals burning flags. It's normally the US Stars and Stripes and is often accompanied by dancing, screaming and the brandishing of long sharp weapons.

Following the broadcast of *Jerry Springer: The Opera* on BBC TV, some Christians decided to publicly burn their TV licence. Or

---

[1] *Father Ted*, Series 1, Episode 3, 1995.

at least a copy of it. This display of disgust at the blasphemy of the broadcast by the BBC is understandable but shocking in a normally mild-mannered British context. The protestors were trying to send a message, but what they were implying was troubling.

Sins and crimes

In Part 1, Chapter 8, we wondered about a comedian in a British comedy club telling a joke that he or she would not tell in public in Tehran, the capital of the theocratic state of Iran. We now live in a world made smaller by smart phones. But we have always had immigration. The UK contains small but growing groups of people who subscribe to various forms of Islam, which tend to respond differently to jokes about blasphemy. We might expect public demonstrations in Muslim countries when *Charlie Hebdo*, for example, published blasphemous cartoons about their prophet. And yet, a mass shooting took place in Paris. Twelve people were shot dead and 11 injured in broad daylight by gunmen who were both born and raised in France.

To the secularized Westerner, the deeds of the killers look like a purely emotional overreaction. But it's not quite that simple. The gunmen were members of an Islamist terror group called Al-Qaeda in the Arabian Peninsula[2] for whom sins against God are essentially crimes. As far as they are concerned, the state should enforce God's law through coercion. What sin could be more serious than blasphemy? In this way of thinking, blasphemers become worthy of death. Many Muslims, of course, would disagree and still say the gunmen's crimes were an overreaction, but the different view of sins and crimes is significant.

This way of thinking might seem alien to us, but it was not an uncommon view in Europe centuries earlier under the Inquisition, for example. It could also be found in twentieth-century Communist states when jokes were made about esteemed leaders.

---

[2] <http://time.com/3661650/charlie-hebdo-paris-terror-attack-al-qaeda/>.

You would not last long in Moscow in the 1940s if you were accused of making a joke at the expense of Joseph Stalin.

But it is still prevalent in the West today, though in an unexpected place. Even if the average Christian in the West does not aspire to a theocratic state, he or she implies that very thing by saying, when grossly offended by a joke about Jesus Christ, 'This should not be allowed.' The expectation is for legal or coercive action, which is tantamount to demanding some kind of theocracy. That is the message sent out by setting fire to TV licences. It says, 'We won't stand for this and something must be done.' But that *something* must be done to *someone*, and carried out with coercive force by the state. In making such demands, these Christians are in danger of confusing the realms of Church and state. They are asking a secular government to enforce God's law.

A radical solution

What are vexed and offended Christians to do? Perhaps they should do something that does not come naturally but might be the wisest course of action: mind their own business. Christians could express their disapproval or displeasure. They could write letters, request their local theatres not to host the production, or stand in the street with a placard, strident or ironic. But what seems harder to justify is demanding that the state punish the unbeliever for the sin of blasphemy.

One theme of the New Testament is to worry more about what's in front of you, your own household and the people around you, rather than to insist everyone else is bent to your will or opinion. In Paul's first letter to the Thessalonians, he writes: 'Aspire to live quietly, and to mind your own affairs, and to work with your hands, as we instructed you, so that you may walk properly before outsiders and be dependent on no one' (1 Thessalonians 4.11–12).

There are many similar verses. The phrase 'As for you' occurs in the Bible many times in relation to ensuring that you don't join in with what everyone else is doing. If everyone around you is blaspheming, make sure that you don't. Through your behaviour you may win the respect of your opponents, who may then listen to what you have to say and even repent of their comments or jokes.

This is not the way of the world today. The media love to whip up and enflame arguments. Ironically, that is the core message of *Jerry Springer: The Opera*. It makes that point rather well. Therefore, allow me to sum up why I didn't add my complaint to the thousands the BBC received about the broadcast of the blasphemous show with this final thought.

Final thought

Jerry Springer: The Opera was broadcast one night in 2005 alongside many other BBC programmes. And I watched it. I found it funny in parts and thought the overall thesis of the satirical show was a good point well made, although the intentionally crass way in which it was done was not quite to my taste. The chorus and music were really good. Some of the language was extremely offensive, as it was designed to be. I was also offended by the inferences being made about Jesus. Personally, as a writer, I have always been uncomfortable putting words into Jesus' mouth, but acknowledge the writers and director do not share my faith or my reluctance to do this.

I did not find myself wanting to watch it again afterwards. Nor do I regret watching it or surrendering to it, as C. S. Lewis suggested I should. I do not feel the need to repent for having seen it, since I don't believe watching it caused me to sin. I don't think the BBC was wrong to broadcast it since it was technically not illegal to do so. Nor should it have been illegal as that creates a worrying confusion of Church and state, and of sins and crimes. I understand that the BBC transmits a range of views, some of which I agree with and some I do not. When I pay my licence fee, I am aware that I am purchasing a range of views.

I also note that the hyperbolic media were uninterested in nuanced opinions and rarely have the time or desire to process them. This rather reinforces the point being made by *Jerry Springer: The Opera.*

Because of all of the above, I did not complain to the BBC, despite being repeatedly urged to do so by leading Christians at the time. I also didn't feel I could complain in advance about something I had not yet seen. Many Christians felt that they should complain, and that they were within their rights to do so. The BBC does respond to feedback and modify its commissioning policies accordingly.

Looking back on the protests and the wider response to *Jerry Springer: The Opera*, it is hard to say that there was any kind of united front. This is because there are many mainstream Christian denominations in the UK, ranging from the Church of England and the Salvation Army to the Elim Pentecostal Church and the Methodists. There are also many voices within those denominations. But sometimes the churches were brought together in opposition to *Jerry Springer: The Opera*. When the touring show came to the Wales Millennium Centre in Cardiff, 100 church leaders signed a letter calling for the show to be withdrawn. The Archbishop of Wales, Barry Morgan, also condemned the staging of the show.[3]

But what happens when a church decides not to set sail into a media storm? And what happens when that show becomes wildly globally successful? We can find out by looking at the story of the critically acclaimed, award-winning, long-running Broadway show, *The Book of Mormon.*

---

[3] <www.christiantoday.com/article/jerry.springer.opens.to.more.protests.in. cardiff/6575.htm>.

27

All-American prophet

W as it divine providence that brought about the Broadway smash hit *The Book of Mormon*? In August 2003, when *South Park* creators Trey Parker and Matt Stone meet Bobby Lopez, it seems a match made in heaven, if you think heaven could have a hand in creating a wildly offensive show like *The Book of Mormon*.

Parker and Stone are working on their puppet-based movie, *Team America: World Police*. They have been told to see Lopez's new puppet-based musical, *Avenue Q*, at the John Golden Theatre on Broadway. When it finishes, Parker thinks, 'This is exactly the thing I've always dreamed of doing.'[1] Lopez was really excited the creators of *South Park* were coming to see his show. Lopez says that when he saw the *South Park* movie he thought, 'This is exactly what I want to be doing.'[2]

When Parker and Stone meet Lopez after the show, they not only get along, they discover that they are all harbouring a desire to do a very specific project: a show based around Joseph Smith and the Mormons.

Eight years later, on 24 March 2011, *The Book of Mormon* opens at the Eugene O'Neill Theatre on Broadway. Fewer than two months later, it scoops nine Tony awards including Best Musical.

---

[1] Trey Lopez, Robert Parker and Matt Stone, *The Book of Mormon: The Testament of a Broadway Musical* (New York: Newmarket Press, 2013), p. 5.

[2] Lopez et al., *The Book of Mormon*, p. 6.

Seven years later, the show is still running on Broadway, along with productions in London, Melbourne and Scandinavia and national tours of the USA.

The gist

The show is not 'the Joseph Smith story', focusing on the founder of Mormonism. Instead, it tells the story of two young modern-day Mormons, Elders Price and Cunningham. They have volunteered to be missionaries for two years, which is normal for serious young Mormons. And Elder Price is serious. Really serious. He wants to change the world for ever and be the best Mormon. Elder Cunningham, on the other hand, is just thrilled that he has a new friend.

They are sent to Uganda where their relentless optimism is quickly dimmed. They find themselves in a very dysfunctional part of the country with an evil child-raping warlord and an Aids epidemic. The locals keep their spirits up by singing a song called '*Hasa Diga Eebowai*' which sounds a lot like '*Hakuna Matata*' from *The Lion King*. Rather than it meaning 'No worries', they explain that '*Hasa Diga Eebowai*' means 'F--- you, God'. Price and Cunningham will have their work cut out.

Price realizes he won't be converting or baptizing anyone soon. This will look bad when they report back to their mission president. Price is devastated, but Cunningham's response is to change the message and tell the locals what they want to hear. This new version of Mormonism, infused with *Lord of the Rings* and *Star Wars*, starts to gain traction. In fact, it becomes so popular that the Mormon mission president comes to visit. The locals put on a traditional Mormon-style pageant to present their comically bastardized version of the religion.

The mission president is horrified by what he sees, and furious. But Price and Cunningham refuse to be chastened for this heresy. They will not go back to the USA when ordered to do so. Crucially, though, they do not reject Mormonism. They decide they can still call themselves Latter-day Saints. They remain in Uganda, where converts now have renewed hope and purpose because of Cunningham's new brand of Mormonism.

Such a brief summary misses out many details, but you can listen to the songs, which account for the vast majority of the show, on streaming music sites like Spotify. You can buy the script or, even better, go and see it for yourself in London, New York or Melbourne. Should you choose to do that, you will see and hear an audience go wild with excitement.

Show-stoppingly funny

Nikki M. James, playing Ugandan villager Nabulungi, was amazed at the reactions to the first public performance of the show. When they sang the '*Hasa Diga*' song and explained the words mean 'F--- you, God', they had to wait in character, or 'vamp', for the audience reaction to die down.

> In rehearsal, we would vamp for a moment. But that night, we're vamping and vamping and vamping, 'cause the audience reaction had this outrageous visceral reaction. They were laughing, they were shocked, they were talking to their friends audibly. We had to just hold and wait. We ended up building a vamp into the show because it still gets a huge, huge laugh. I'd never heard a laugh like it in all my years of musical comedy. It literally stops the show cold while the audience sort of collects itself, and then we can move on.[3]

Critics were broadly positive about the show, but not universally so. Even positive reviews, such as Charles McNulty's in the *Los Angeles Times*, were tempered with suggestions that the plot was faltering and that the first act ended with a whimper, before concluding, 'Sure it's crass, but the show is not without

---

[3] Lopez et al., *The Book of Mormon*, p. 47.

good intentions and, in any case, vindicates itself with musical panache.'[4]

Minority faith

Before we look at the Mormon response, we need to look at how Parker, Stone and Lopez succeeded in bringing a minority faith into the comedy mainstream. The Church of Latter-day Saints claims a global membership of just over 16 million, of whom 6.6 million live in the USA.[5] That's only 1 in 45 Americans, or about 2 per cent of the population. The remaining 10 million are scattered across the world. This is certainly a minority faith.

In Part 2, Chapter 19, of this book, we noted that it's very hard to make jokes about various strands of Islam when the details of that faith are not widely known. But Mormonism seems to have a greater cultural footprint than the numbers initially suggest. First, the religion has a strong base in the state of Utah. The capital, Salt Lake City, is not large but was significant enough to host the 2002 Winter Olympics. The following year, Parker and Stone felt there was sufficient recognition to base an entire episode of *South Park* around the faith. 'All About Mormons' aired on 19 November 2003 as part of Season 7. The spotlight was thrown on Mormonism again in 2008 when Mitt Romney was the Republican nomination to run for US president against Barack Obama.

By 2011, Mormonism was a significant cultural phenomenon, providing sufficient stereotypes for comedy to exploit. Broadway was ready for a musical about Mormonism.

Before even entering the theatre, the audience of the show could see a Mormon stereotype emblazoned on the publicity and posters: the clean-cut look of a young white man in black trousers, white shirt and black tie.

---

[4] <http://latimesblogs.latimes.com/culturemonster/2011/03/theater-review-the-book-of-mormon-at-the-eugene-oneill-theatre.html>.

[5] <www.mormonnewsroom.org/facts-and-statistics/country/united-states>.

When the show starts, we are quickly into a song about Mormons doing another familiar activity that we associate with them: ringing your doorbell and offering you a book they say will change your life. Specific, lesser-known information about Joseph Smith and the Golden Plates is neatly explained as the show goes along – before being lampooned.

The secret of the show's success

The show has been a huge box-office hit. How did it turn out to be not only possible but highly successful? Some have argued the reason is the show's resonance far beyond Mormonism. In *Singing and Dancing to The Book of Mormon*, Sirvent and Baker say that the

> object of Parker and Stone's satire is . . . something far more pervasive than the Mormon Church itself – indeed, their criticisms ultimately seem to be directed not at a people of a particular faith but of a particular mindset.[6]

There is some evidence to support this assertion. One song in particular, 'I Believe', is sung by Elder Price, who demonstrates that being a Mormon is an act of willpower and self-delusion. But is this song about *all* religions requiring blind faith? 'Turn It Off' shows how Mormons are trained to be inherently self-denying and are therefore dehumanized. Don't other religions teach followers to deny self? Jesus himself says, 'If anyone would come after me, let him deny himself and take up his cross daily and follow me' (Luke 9.23).

Sirvent and Baker point to the '*Hasa Diga*' song, suggesting 'thoughtful audience members may even conclude that the most offensive aspect of "*Hasa Diga Eebowai*" is not the blasphemy of

---

[6] Roberto Sirvant and Neil Baker, 'Reinhold Niebuhr and religious foolishness', in *Singing and Dancing to The Book of Mormon: Critical Essays on the Broadway Musical*, ed. Marc Edward Shaw and Holly Welker (London: Rowman and Littlefield, 2016), ch. 4, p. 43.

Ugandans but the theology of missionaries!' Undoubtedly, the visceral audience response to that song, which so took actress Nikki M. James by surprise, is not celebrating the evisceration of the Mormon God, known as Heavenly Father. The joke is not 'F--- you, Heavenly Father'. It's 'F--- you, God'.

Has this anti-religion theme struck a chord in a post-religious Western culture? Are Parker, Stone and Lopez pointing their finger not just at Mormonism but at all theistic forms of religion? Mormons aren't the only ones in the dock here. They need to make room for all adherents to any dogmatic faith that claims God is real and good, when such suffering is allowed to happen in places like Uganda.[7]

Sirvent and Baker's opinion is also shared by a popular writer for the *New York Times*, David Brooks, who wrote that the 'central theme of *The Book of Mormon* is that many religious stories are silly – the idea that God would plant golden plates in upstate New York. Many religious doctrines are rigid and out of touch.'[8]

Man the barricades

Should all religions feel equally wounded and affronted by this show? Should mainstream Protestants, as well as Mormons, Catholics, Baptists and Christadelphians, dust off their placards and start marching around in small circles outside the Prince of Wales Theatre in the West End? Should the Prince of Wales, the future Governor of the Church of England, not suggest the theatre that bears his name distance itself from the show?

---

[7] Ironically, a place where a joke would not have same effect is Uganda, where the vast majority of people practise or adhere to a religious faith of some kind. According to a 2014 census, only 0.2 per cent of the population claim to have no religion. See: <www.ubos.org/onlinefiles/uploads/ubos/NPHC/2014%20National%20Census%20Main%20Report.pdf>. The depiction of the Ugandans is one of the more troubling and morally ambiguous aspects of the show.

[8] <www.nytimes.com/2011/04/22/opinion/22brooks.html?_r=0>.

Moreover, Jesus is personified in *The Book of Mormon*, as he is in *Jerry Springer: The Opera*, saying things he doesn't say in the Bible. In *The Book of Mormon*, he appears in Elder Price's 'Spooky Mormon Hell Dream', and accuses Elder Price of being 'a dick'. Shouldn't that be enough to spark protests, petitions and private prosecutions?

The wider Christian Church did not engage with the show in this way. There may be a couple of reasons. The first is that mainstream Christian denominations tend to see Mormonism as a deviation from any kind of recognizable Christianity. The Mormon faith no longer affirms the Trinity, and although it accepts the Bible as inspired (when translated correctly), greater significance is attached to the *Book of Mormon, Doctrine and Covenants* and the *Pearl of Great Price*. These officially recognized canon books, Christians might argue, are difficult to reconcile with standard Christian doctrine. Defending Mormonism in public could suggest that Mormons are closer to mainstream Christianity than is deemed desirable.

The main reason there was not a *Jerry Springer: The Opera*-style media storm of outrage and indignation from Christian churches is because the Mormons themselves did not seem too upset. The Church of Latter-day Saints even took out adverts in the programme of the show, suggesting the audience, having seen the stage show, read the original book for themselves. There have been reports of people becoming Mormons through watching the show.[9]

The Church of Latter-day Saints' official statement on the show in 2011 was as follows: 'The production may attempt to entertain audiences for an evening, but the Book of Mormon as a volume of scripture will change people's lives forever by bringing them closer to Christ.'

---

[9] <www.deseretnews.com/article/865687833/Musical-to-missionary-How-Broadways-Book-of-Mormon--led-teen-to-serve-LDS-mission.html>.

It's a neat statement and very Mormon in its politeness. Note they do not say the show is entertaining, but that entertainment is merely being attempted. Since that statement was issued, nothing else has been said publicly, other than private suggestions to faithful Mormons that they should not go to see the show. Overall, many Mormons were proud of the way their church publicly responded the show.[10]

Second opinion

So is that the end of the matter? Is there nothing to see here? If the Mormon Church is not offended, why continue the discussion? Plenty of Mormons were offended by the show, as were many non-Mormons. But a closer examination of the show would suggest the Mormons in particular were right to be offended.

The notion that the show is an attack on religion in general doesn't quite hold up. As we noted earlier, when Parker, Stone and Lopez met, they all agreed they wanted to do a show about Joseph Smith and Mormonism, rather than religion in general. (The show is fairly pro-faith, as long as it makes people feel good and makes the world a better place.) Plenty of jokes are made at the expense of the Mormon faith, which encourages Latter-day Saints not to ask questions but simply believe. Although this charge can be made against numerous religions, this show pins it firmly on Mormons. And it rings true.

The more subtle criticism of Mormonism can be seen in how Elder Cunningham makes up his own version of Mormonism and a new form of Mormonism is born. Is he a kind of Joseph Smith figure? Is the suggestion that Joseph Smith and his successors were simply making it up as they went along? There's a hint of that in the 'I Believe' song, in which Price sings: 'I believe that in

10 <www.deseretnews.com/article/865686543/Readers-share-thoughts-on-The-Book-of-Mormon-musical-returning-to-Salt-Lake-City.html>.

1978 God changed his mind about black people.'[11] Other things that Mormons are required to believe without question are also listed.

The implication of the show is that Mormonism is simply a religion born from the imagination of a man. That same religion responds to questions and doubts with demands to simply believe more. If you have doubts or conflicting feelings, 'Turn It Off'. If you're feeling overwhelmed, 'Man Up'. And if you think about disobeying or leaving the faith, you will have a 'Spooky Mormon Hell Dream'. The song 'All-American Prophet' seems to draw some of these themes together. Put like this, the theme of the show doesn't seem very subtle at all. This show is surely offensive to Mormons?

The response of the Church of Jesus Christ of Latter-day Saints, however, was wise. And very Mormon. If they felt distressed or upset, they didn't show it. They suppressed it, smiled sweetly and moved on. But the Mormons also have confidence in their own theological system. They are sure they will be proved right in the end when we all meet our Maker.[12]

Christian confidence

This is why Christians could and should have been more gracious in relation to *Jerry Springer: The Opera*. Christians should not need feel the need to scream, shout and sue if God is truly in charge. A quick survey of the Bible would suggest that God achieves his purposes and plans in spite of human help, rather than because of it.

---

[11] A Mormon, of course, would not put it like this. And for Mormons, God changing his mind tends to be a good thing, rather than something theologically problematic. See: <time.com/3905811/mormon-priesthood-men-women-integration/>.

[12] In Mormon theology, the afterlife options are more varied than the standard heaven or hell.

Some Christians may think that I am not sufficiently zealous for the honour of God's name. They may point to the Gospel accounts of Jesus with a whip in the Temple overturning the tables, because he was jealous for the holiness of God's name. It is a remarkable event, made all the more so because it is such a rare event in the life of Christ.

Moreover, Jesus *is* competent to judge with a whip and, I believe, will judge the world. But I need to be very careful in how I wield physical force or invite others to do so. It is striking what Jesus did when accused of blasphemy, which is a funny accusation given he was actually God. He did not plead his case or fight his corner. He walked away. And when they arrested him, even though he could summon a host of angels to carry him away, he was silent and accepted the unjust punishment.

In fact, in many ways, Easter is a very comic event, as we shall see in our final chapter.

28

What's so funny about Easter?

Here's something that sounds like a joke but isn't:
When is a joke not a joke?
When it's an April fool.

I told you it wasn't a joke. It's not funny. But then again, neither is April Fool's Day. You will detect a mild note of disapprobation in my tone here. I'm not a fan of April Fool's Day, mainly because, as you have discovered, I'm boringly technical about comedy. Practical jokes aren't jokes. They are pranks. They are hoaxes. Not jokes.

Having read almost of all of this book, you know why practical jokes are not really jokes. Jokes require shared information. But if you are being pranked, either by an individual or by a national newspaper, you don't have all the information. If you're being pranked by a schoolboy in a black-and-white Will Hay film, you don't know he's put a bucket of water above the door. You aren't in on the joke. You are part of the joke. In fact, you are the joke.

Thinking bigger

The dynamic shifts when we scale this up to a full-blown hoax. This is the favoured April Fool gag of the moment. Newspapers, radio breakfast shows and large corporations love to tell a story that is on the edge of believability but is actually pure fiction. In 2017, Emirates airline announced its triple-decker plane, complete with swimming pool, games room and park. A year earlier, the Texas Comptroller of Public Accounts tweeted that Texas would start to issue its own currency. In 2014, King's College Choir in Cambridge announced that they were replacing boys singing soprano with older men using helium instead. They produced an amusing video illustrating this.

In these cases, an enormous bucket of water is being placed on a huge doorway in order to drench an entire nation. Only the perpetrator of the hoax has all the facts. The rest of us are not in on the joke. We are all the joke. Anyone who 'falls for it' is the joke. And rather than getting wet, you feel foolish. How is that a joyful comic experience? The hoax then is not a joke. It's a prank. This is why I'm not a fan of April Fool's Day. Thank you for listening.

Easter tomfoolery

What does this have to do with Easter other than taking place at roughly the same time of year? In 2018, Easter Day fell on April Fool's Day for the first time since 1956.[1] Sceptics of the Christian faith may have enjoyed this coincidence since they might be tempted to describe Easter as another day in which Christians are taken in by what must be a hoax. They argue, not unreasonably, that the dead do not come back to life.[2] I would argue that this is the very point of the story. The dead do not rise. But Jesus did.

Taking the story of the death of Jesus at face value, it doesn't seem like a comic tale. The Church rarely presents it as such. But it used to. The phrase *Risus Paschalis* could be found in Easter celebrations in previous centuries. It means 'the Easter laugh'.

---

[1] It will happen again in 2029 (by which time I hope to be able to relaunch this book as some kind of retinal scan or brain implant). It happens once more in 2040, and then not for another 130 years.

[2] Let's not get into that here. Many books have been written on the subject, like Norman Anderson's *Evidence for the Resurrection* (London: Inter-Varsity Fellowship, 1950) or Lee Strobel's *The Case for Easter* (Grand Rapids, Michigan: Zondervan, 1998).

Advanced joking

Easter laughter

The origin of the phrase *Risus Paschalis* is obscure. Some attribute it to early Church Fathers like Gregory of Nyssa.[3] There is stronger evidence of linking Easter with comedy in the work of Christian philosopher Peter Abelard (1079–1142). He wrote hymns for Good Friday and Holy Saturday, asking God to allow the faithful to enjoy the 'laugh of Easter grace'.[4]

On the eve of the Reformation in the early sixteenth century, it had become a widespread phenomenon. Priests would tell jokes in Easter sermons. These attracted criticism from Luther's contemporaries, Oecolampadius and Erasmus, who were shocked by the bawdiness and tone of the gags, which they considered unsuitable for church.

What's the joke?

To those outside the Church, and plenty inside, it may not be easy to see what the big joke is about Easter. In bald terms, God tricked Satan. Since the fall of humanity in the Garden of Eden, God had been working on a plan to save people from their sin. This is hinted at many times in the Bible in passages like Isaiah 53 (normally read in carol services). We also get the bizarre gift of myrrh, for embalming, at Jesus' birth.

In contriving the death of Jesus, Satan achieved God's purposes. Jesus saved the world by his death on the cross and Old Nick was humiliated by Jesus' resurrection on the third day.

---

[3] But these early Christian fathers were not known for their sense of humour. In 390, John Chrysostom (c. 347–407) preached, 'This world is not a theatre in which we can laugh, and we are not assembled in order to burst into peals of laughter, but to weep for our sins.' Clement of Alexandria and Augustine were also suspicious of humour, just as the Church is today.

[4] Michael O'Connell, 'Mockery, farce and *Risus Paschalis* in the York Christ before Herod', in *Farce and Farcical Elements*, edited by Wim N. M. Hüsken Konrad Schoell and Leif Søndergaard (Amsterdam: Rodopi, 2002), p. 48.

God 1: Lucifer 0. Laugh at the devil. He's been played for a fool. In fact, he's an eternal April Fool.

The devil in the detail

The *Risus Paschalis* tradition waned for a variety of reasons.[5] It may have fallen by the wayside because of theological shifts in the past 500 years. As with mystery plays, the Reformation has something to answer for here.

But Easter is funny in other ways, even though it does not seem so at first or possibly even second glance. Crucifixion is a gruesome and painful punishment. (It is literally excruciating. That's where the word comes from.) It would therefore seem hard to describe the brutal execution of any man – let alone the God–Man Jesus Christ – as funny.

A fresh look at the details of the story, however, reveals a story riddled with comic incongruities and ironies. This begins well before the traditionally recognized Passion narratives. We have already seen in Part 2, Chapter 16, how Jesus' raising of Lazarus creates comedy back at the Temple in John 11. On seeing that Jesus has power over life and death, the religious authorities decide to kill him.

This is quite a contrast from the numerous occasions where Jesus predicts his own death, like Mark 9.30–32. The disciples have no idea what he meant since, in their minds, there was no way this miracle worker could be killed.

False sense of security

Killing Jesus, however, proved worryingly easy, considering his divine, cosmic power. His trial was rushed and fixed. The crowd were so easily swayed. They had been cheering Jesus' triumphal entry into Jerusalem and there they were, demanding the release of a murderer. The speed with which they spoke with one

---

[5] You can read some of those reasons here: <www.jamescary.co.uk/church/christianity/whats-funny-easter/>.

collective mind is reminiscent of the 'Yes, we are all individuals' scene in Monty Python's *Life of Brian*.

Black Friday

In the blackest and bleakest day in human history, all of the above mocked and jeered as Jesus was nailed to a cross beneath a sign saying that he was the king of the Jews, which is funny because it's true. The only person who had committed no sin was crucified between two common criminals. One of the criminals, despite being near to death himself, used his dying words to join the mockers, sneering at Jesus. The other is told by Jesus they will be together in paradise (Luke 23.43). Likewise, a centurion, the despised Roman occupier, could see that this man was the Son of God (Mark 15.39). Meanwhile, Peter, the sturdy fisherman, Jesus' rock, who has been with him for a few years, is denying him to a young girl. In a way, this is more humiliating than the experience of disciple who runs away naked in the Garden of Gethsemane (Mark 14.52).

Ironies abound as the religious people mishear Jesus quoting Psalm 22, saying, 'He is calling Elijah' when he is giving more clues to his identity and the awful mistake the religious leaders have made. They taunt Jesus, telling him to come down from the cross, which he could do but chooses not to. 'He saved others; he cannot save himself' (Matthew 27.42). He is, of course, saving others at the cost of his own life. Jesus, the Prince of Peace, healer of the sick, God's chosen, prophesied king, has been killed by priests. It doesn't get more incongruous than that.

Death, where is thy sting?

The Easter story was not over. The disciples had missed the clues which were not very subtle. The earth had shaken. Rocks had split open. There was an unexpected total solar eclipse that lasted not minutes but hours. Three hours. The tall, thick, woven tapestry curtain from the Temple, protecting the Holy of Holies, was torn in half. From top to bottom. Then a zombie apocalypse. 'The tombs were also opened. And many bodies of the saints who had fallen asleep were raised, and coming out of the tombs after his resurrection they went into the holy city and appeared to many' (Matthew 27.52). The signs were there that something of cosmic significance was happening.

Jesus' followers seemed convinced that when Jesus said, 'It is finished', it really was finished. When the women brought spices to the tomb on the Sunday, they were not planning to use them to make celebratory herbal tea. The spices were for Jesus' corpse. But his tomb was empty. The body was gone. Disciples were summoned. Angels reminded them of Jesus' words, pointing out how embarrassingly clear Jesus had been about what would happen when he was killed.

This is the moment of triumph. Jesus saved his best miracle until last. Euphoria. Joy. Jubilation. Laughter. Death is defeated. The priests, the principalities, the powers and Pontius Pilate have been thwarted. Jesus wins.

What happened next?

The Easter comedy continues and becomes more obvious in the scene that follows in Luke 24. Two followers of Jesus, possibly Cleopas and his wife, are on the way to Emmaus when they meet Jesus. Except they don't realize it is him. But we do. (Hurray for shared information!) The two followers are astonished that the man they have met is ignorant of what's been happening in recent days. They have the temerity to say to Jesus, 'Are you the only visitor to Jerusalem who does not know the things that have happened there in these days?' (v. 18). Now that's funny.

It gets funnier when they proceed to mansplain everything to the Supreme Being. But it turns out the man they've met knows way more about it than they thought. He rebukes the two followers before Godsplaining everything to them. They beg this stranger to stay and eat with them, and when he breaks the bread, they recognize him. And he vanishes.

The two followers run miles back to Jerusalem, saying that they've seen the risen Christ. One can imagine the disbelief in the room, and how their attempts to be convincing are vindicated when Jesus himself appears. The scene that unfolds is undoubtedly comic, especially when one really imagines how the disciples must have been feeling. The disciples are in a state of shock, fear, confusion and joy.

Blithe spirits

The scene we find at the end of Luke's Gospel, with Jesus appearing to the disciples, is a bit of a comedy staple. You will find it in films and plays, like Ricky Gervais' overlooked comedy *Ghost Town* and Noel Coward's *Blithe Spirit*. In the latter, an eccentric medium is invited to conduct a séance by a novelist looking for material for a book. It backfires when the medium invokes the spirit of the novelist's annoying and temperamental first wife, Elvira, and the comedy plays out from there.

This kind of comedy is not just to be found in Edwardian spiritualism. You'll find something similar if you look up the astonishing scene in 1 Samuel 28 with the witch of Endor. Saul wishes to speak with Samuel to gain wisdom and prophecy about a forthcoming battle. Except Samuel is dead. When Samuel was alive, Saul didn't listen to a word he said. But now Samuel is long dead, Saul is all ears. More irony.

In order to hear a prophetic man of God, a God who has forbidden sorcery and witchcraft, King Saul pays a visit to the witch of Endor. The king goes in disguise, obviously, but the witch sees through it when Saul asks for Samuel. (Margaret Rutherford from *Blithe Spirit* would make an excellent witch in this scene.) But the séance continues and Samuel actually appears. He issues the same prophecy that he'd been prophesying all his life – the very one that Saul refused to listened to – but here's the kicker: Samuel signs off by saying that Saul and his sons will be joining him in the afterlife tomorrow. Ouch. But funny.

And here's the kicker

Let us return to the scene at the end of Luke's Gospel where they all 'disbelieved with joy and were marvelling' (Luke 24.41). At that moment, Jesus says something hilarious: 'Have you anything to eat?' It really punctures the moment. Clearly Jesus is keen to prove that he is not merely an apparition or a spirit, but that his resurrection body is physical and real. But the moment is comic.

There is a very similar joke in terms of the incongruity of cosmic wonder and earthly banality in Terry Pratchett's finest work, *Mort*. The young Mort meets Death in order to be his apprentice and it's a very funny scene. (Death speaks in capital letters, by the way.)

'It's beautiful,' said Mort, softly. 'What is it?'
THE SUN IS UNDER THE DISC, said Death.
'Is it like this every night?'
EVERY NIGHT, said Death. NATURE'S LIKE THAT.
'Doesn't anyone know?'
ME. YOU. THE GODS. GOOD, ISN'T IT?
'Gosh!'
Death leaned over the saddle and looked down at the kingdoms of the world.
I DON'T KNOW ABOUT YOU, he said, BUT I COULD MURDER A CURRY.[6]

One could read Jesus' request for food in this way. They give him broiled fish, and you imagine them gawping at him as he eats it, to see what will happen. Throughout the Gospels, we see people trying to come to terms with the man who is God. Here, we see them processing how a dead man can be alive. Such a scene is hard to play any other way than comically.

[6] Terry Pratchett, *Mort* (London: Victor Gollancz, 1987), p. 25.

Easter tomfoolery

The Easter story brings all of these astonishing incongruities crashing together into a comic and cosmic symphony. They are interwoven through the Bible, stunning in their complexity and yet their overall message is so sweet and simple it can scarcely be believed. Christ is risen! Hallelujah!

Risus Paschalis is, and should still be, part of the Christian tradition. Any tradition that makes Christians laugh more and see the comedy that God has woven into the text of the Bible and the fabric of the universe would be very welcome.

The sacred art of joking

In Eco's *The Name of the Rose*, Jorge commits murder in order to prevent Aristotle's second *Poetics* book about comedy from being discovered, translated and read. For him, comedy is so subversive that it only brings anarchy, disrespect and godlessness. Jorge is prepared to burn the book – and destroy the entire library in which it has been hidden – rather than allow anyone to discover the secrets of laughter. He is a truly tragic figure, but one who would feel at home in many Christian churches and communities today. He'd be great on Twitter.

Too often, we fail to appreciate the absurdities and incongruities found throughout Scripture, buried even within the darkest of tales like the Easter story. We are often naïve and short-sighted in our handling of conflicts surrounding jokes. We judge jokes in the wrong way, robbing them of their context and listening only to the shrieks of offence taken or feigned.

Psalm 2 says that, in heaven, God is laughing at us. All things considered, that seems a highly appropriate response to our pomposity and self-importance. We think we can fully understand the sacred art of joking, but we don't and we can't. We simply don't have all the information. But God does. We are April Fools. In fact, we are Year-Round Clowns. When all is said and done, the joke's on all of us. So we might as well have a good laugh.